PHYSICAL CHILDREN, ACTIVE TEACHING
Investigating physical literacy

Patricia Maude

Open University Press
Buckingham • Philadelphia

Open University Press
Celtic Court
22 Ballmoor
Buckingham
MK18 1XW

email: enquiries@openup.co.uk
world wide web: www.openup.co.uk

and

325 Chestnut Street
Philadelphia, PA 19106, USA

First Published 2001

A catalogue record of this book is available from the British Library

ISBN   0 335 20573 9 (hb)   0 335 20572 0 (pb)

Library of Congress Cataloging-in-Publication Data
Maude, Patricia.
   Physical children, active teaching: investigating physical
literacy / Patricia Maude.
      p.   cm. – (Enriching the primary curriculum – child, teacher, context).
   Includes bibliographical references and index.
      ISBN 0–335–20573–9 – ISBN 0–335–20572–0 (pbk.)
      1. Physical education for children – Study and teaching
(Elementary) – Great Britain.   2. Movement education – Study and
teaching (Elementary) – Great Britain.   I. Title.   II. Series.
GV443 .M34 2001
372.86'0941–dc21   00–050154

Typeset by Graphicraft Limited, Hong Kong
Printed in Great Britain by The Cromwell Press, Trowbridge

Contents

List of figures and tables

Figures

Tables

Series editor's preface

Cameo

Glenn has taught across the age range in different primary
schools for the last 15 years, specializing in art. In that time,
he has had to make many adjustments in his thinking. The
emphasis now appears to have shifted significantly from
considering the learning needs of children as paramount, to
'delivering' a curriculum over which he feels little ownership
and about which he feels even less real enthusiasm! The
National Curriculum, with its individual subjects and language
of 'teaching', not to mention an impending Office for Standards
in Education (Ofsted) inspection, has shaken his confidence
somewhat in his own understanding of what primary education
is all about. It has also meant that he feels *he* is doing most of
the learning, rather than the children – all those detailed plans
and topic packs for individual subjects which teachers have
been developing within the school seem to Glenn to leave little
for children to actually do except explore the occasional
artefact and fill in worksheets.

Yet he knows that he enjoys the 'buzz' of teaching, revels in
being part of children's progress and achievements, delights
in those rare times when he can indulge in art activities
with children, is appreciated by parents and colleagues for the
quality of his work and, generally, still finds his real heart lies
in being an educator and doing something worthwhile. His
constant question to himself is 'How can I work with children
in ways I feel and *know* are appropriate and yet meet the
outside demands made on me?'

Sound familiar? You may well begin to recognize a 'Glenn' within you! He encapsulates the way many teachers are feeling at the present time and the persistent doubts and uncertainties which continually underpin many teachers' work. In the early and middle years of primary schooling in particular, teachers are facing great challenges in conceiving how best to accommodate the learning needs of children in a context of growing pressure, innovation and subject curriculum demand. Yet conscientiousness drives the professional to strive for greater understanding – that little bit more knowledge or skill might just make a big difference to one child, or it might provide improved insights into one aspect of the curriculum.

Glenn, like many teachers, needs time, encouragement and support to reflect on his current practice and to consider in an objective way the changes needed. Rather than trying to add something else to an already overcrowded curriculum, today's teachers should consider those existing aspects which are fundamental to ensuring that children are not only schooled but educated in the broadest possible sense. Only then can we begin to sort out those things which are vital, those things we would like to do, and those things which would benefit from a rethink.

This series aims to offer practitioners food for thought as well as practical and theoretical support in establishing, defining and refining their own understandings and beliefs. It focuses particularly on enriching curriculum experiences for everyone through recognizing and appreciating the crucial interface between the child, the teacher and the context of primary education, including the curriculum context. Each title in the series seeks collectively and individually to enhance teachers' understanding about the theories which underpin, guide and enrich quality practice in a range of broader curriculum aspects, while acknowledging issues such as class size and overload, common across primary schools today.

Each book operates from the basis of exploring teachers' sound – frequently intuitive – experiences and understanding of teaching and learning processes and outcomes which most teachers inevitably possess in good measure and which, like Glenn, they often feel constrained to use. For example, the editor is regularly told by teachers and others in primary schools that they 'know' or 'feel' that play for children is or must be a valuable process, yet they are also aware that this is not often reflected in their

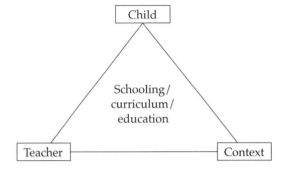

Figure 1   Child, teacher, context

planning or curriculum management and that the context of education generally is antithetical to play. What is more, they really do not know what to do about it and find articulating the justification for play practices extremely difficult. Other writers in the series have suggested that this is also the case in their areas of expertise.

All the books in this series seek to enrich and extend teachers' curriculum thinking beyond the level of just 'subjects', into dimensions related to the teaching and learning needs of children and the contextual demands faced by schools. The books cover areas such as creativity, success and competence, exploration and problem solving, information technology across subjects and boundaries, play in the primary curriculum, questioning and teacher–child interactions, values in relation to equality issues, social, moral and spiritual frameworks, and physical aspects of teaching and learning. Each book has had, within its working title, the rationale of the unique triad of child, teacher and context which underpins all primary schooling and education, for example in this particular case, interaction and communication. This structure serves to emphasize for authors the inextricable and imperative balance in this triad for effective classroom and curriculum practices. The model we have developed and agreed is shown in Figure 1.

All the writers in the series have been concerned to emphasize the quality, nature and extent of existing classroom practices, and how it is possible to build on these sound pedagogical bases. For this reason, chapters within each title often begin with two or more cameos offering features of practice as starting points for teasing out aspects requiring enquiry, analysis, evaluation and discussion. Chapters then develop their own relevant themes but with consistent reference to what these mean to children and teachers within the general autonomy, and constraints, of the school context.

Issues concerning the *child* take their stance from cognitive psychology (as this book does) and include the child as:

- an active searcher after meaning;
- an individual with particular perceptions of the world and their part in it;
- a person who can reflect on their own learning and understanding;
- a learner with his or her own curriculum needs and interests to be considered;
- an interactive person, learning in collaboration with peers and adults;
- a unique individual but also one with collective needs;
- a member of a 'social' community, i.e. home, family, school, wider community.

Aspects to do with the teaching role lay stress on the *teacher* as a reflective and critical professional who will occasionally but regularly need to stand back from day-to-day practice in order to think about and analyse the triadic relationships and to acknowledge:

- their own learning styles and experiences;
- their own beliefs, values, knowledge and conceptual understanding of pedagogy;
- their need to raise questions about practice and find solutions in an ongoing way;
- their role as mutual learners with children and colleagues;
- their responsibilities as facilitators of learning, as models of learning and as negotiators of meaning with children;
- their role in enabling children's learning rather than always in 'teaching';
- their function as observers and assessors of children's understandings as well as outcomes;
- their obligation clearly to conceptualize the whole curriculum of which the National Curriculum is a part.

When we consider the *context* of pedagogy, this focus subsumes such aspects as the learning environment, school ethos and the actual classroom and school. It also includes such elements as:

- the physical environment – indoors and outdoors;
- the social environment of school and schooling (e.g. is the child an outcome of the context or has the context influenced the child?);
- the psychological environment of school and schooling;
- the philosophical considerations within schools and aspects such as teachers' beliefs and values;
- the curriculum context, including the National Curriculum where this is relevant and appropriate, but also showing where this does not necessarily meet pedagogical needs;
- the frameworks within which the whole concept of schooling takes place and where this fits education in a broader sense.

The overall rationale for each book in the series starts from a belief that teachers should be enabled to analyse their own practices in specific aspects of the broader curriculum as a major aspect of their professionalism. The books are particularly useful at a time of continual curriculum change, when reflection is being focused back upon the child and pedagogy generally as the only perpetuating and consistent elements.

As an integral component, all the books weave teachers' assessment of children's learning and understanding into each particular focus, the intention being to show how the planning> learning>assessment>planning cycle is vital to the quality and success of children's and teachers' learning experiences. With their practical ideas, challenges and direct relevance to classroom practice, these books offer ways of establishing theory as *the* adjunct to practice; they build on teachers' thinking about how they already work in the classroom and help teachers to consider how they may enrich, extend and advance their practices to the mutual benefit of themselves, the children, the curriculum and education in society as a whole.

Physical children, active teaching is a book to support and inspire practitioners involved in movement education with all 3- to 11-year-old children. Through delightful cameos and pacey writing, Trish Maude uses her undeniable enthusiasm, commitment and tremendous depth of knowledge about physical development and human movement to show just what physical education should mean for children and teachers. The whole book is full of life, joy and exuberance – just what physical education and 'growing up' in itself should be like.

Those of you who perhaps have never made the most of those timetabled hall or outdoor PE sessions, or have perceived there to be too many other 'important' things to do in curriculum time, should read this book closely. Trish highlights and pinpoints the vital links between movement education in all its forms and thinking skills, literacy development, creativity and maths – essentially all areas of the National Curriculum as well as the Early Learning Goals. She describes the process as being 'physically educated' and outlines it as a key factor underpinning all areas of learning. Teachers must work in tandem with children to encourage and develop the highest quality physical skills and understanding. Throughout the six chapters, Trish provides teachers with a useful and formative rationale for engaging children physically in order to encourage delight in their own movement capabilities and 'learning with the body' (Chapter 2), improve literacy learning and creative skills (Chapter 3) and engage in well formulated observation and assessment activities (Chapter 4).

Other chapters take further strength from the clear arguments presented as to why more static activities are developmentally so inappropriate for all 3- to 11-year-olds. 'Sitting still' is described as associated with the hardest physical task of all – stillness – and Trish emphasizes that children who cannot sit still are often the ones who need *more* rather than less physical activity. It is vital that we're not so busy 'delivering' the curriculum that we forget our physical learners! No child should 'be hindered from learning an academic skill . . . on account of an underdeveloped motor skill' (Chapter 1). Readers are encouraged to remember that 'movement precedes spoken language developmentally as a medium for communication and retains its key role throughout the primary years'. Play, the focus of Chapter 2, has similar emphasis.

There are many, many ways in which this book is a delight, one of which is that it 'goes against the grain' in relation to what might be conceived of as traditional thinking about physical education. I was constantly delighted in reading through the text that things I had taken as 'givens' were continually challenged and new ideas presented. One of these worth mentioning here is the old educational adage 'You can't talk and perform'! These days are decidedly over and Trish argues with great clarity that talk is vital to the movement process and is one aspect of enabling children to develop what she calls 'physical literacy'. The special place of dance in enabling children to interpret language into thought and action is underlined in Chapter 5, together with other, sometimes underused, aspects of the movement curriculum, e.g. games, gymnastics, swimming and athletics. The argument for providing a full range of such activities for children is forcefully made and an unambiguous rationale presented to support teachers in exploring these aspects with parents and others who need to understand about inclusion of these crucial curriculum aspects.

Every chapter provides insight and guidance into a range of varied and stimulating physical activities that teachers can take up and use immediately. Like all the writers in the series, Trish has managed to pack a wealth of information and passion into relatively few pages that are accessible and capable of having immediate impact on teaching.

Trish weaves her arguments skilfully around the three themes of child, teacher and context, emphasizing each differentially within separate chapters in a book that I know all teachers will find informative, refreshing and vital to their role in providing not only for children's education but for their physical and mental well-being too.

Janet Moyles

Acknowledgements

Inspiration gained from the many children with whom I have worked in schools and in Homerton Gymnastics Club.

The encouragement and support of family and friends.

The help of the staff and children of Norwich Road Primary School, Romsey Junior School, Sedley Infant School, Stapleford Primary School and members of Homerton Gymnastics Club, who participated to provide the photographs.

The Youth Sport Trust, John Sumpter Photography and Mike Whiting, for the photographs of BT TOP Sport and Ecclesiastical TOP Link.

Motor development in infants (p. 7) from *Understanding Child Development* by Spencer A. Rathus (1988: 202) is reproduced by permission of Holt, Rinehart and Winston, Inc., Orlando.

Developmental sequence in running (p. 17) from *Understanding Motor Development* by David L. Gallahue (1989: 238) is reproduced by permission of WCB Brown and Benchmark, Dubuque.

Introduction

Having been an enthusiastic supporter of physical education (PE) from my childhood, including those daily 'drill' sessions, it is a great joy to keep on discovering, when talking with children, that they have just the same lively enthusiasm for the subject as I had then and still have now. Our local primary school had not embarked upon what was then known as the new-style PE, so we had daily physical training (PT) sessions on the playground and very thorough training it was, too. To this day I can remember the importance impressed upon us of copying the teacher's movements accurately and of standing up straight, with correct posture, in between the exercises. We learnt Greek dancing too, which, we were told, was also good for posture. I remember how tiring it was to have to pretend to be carrying an urn on our heads! In the summer we had a sports day, with ribbons as prizes for winning races. In secondary school we did gymnastics, hockey, tennis and swimming. Does one ever forget the exuberant anticipation that preceded each swimming lesson? What I did not realize until recently is that children today experience just the same excitement at the prospect of their PE lessons. It was when listening to children talking about their PE learning during their interviews for the *Gym Kit* video (Maude 1994) that I realized just how articulate and observant children can be. Paul, aged 10, says of his learning in gymnastics: 'I've learnt a lot from Anna and Charlotte, about keeping my legs straight when I do a cartwheel. My legs used to be all over the place, but now I know how to keep my knees and ankles straight!' The children give detailed accounts both of their own and of their peers' work. They are able to observe closely and give positive as well as developmental feedback. They also have an empathy with each other's work in a way that could not be achieved by a teacher.

The inspiration for this book, then, is a dedication to the continued provision of physical education that engages children in that excitement and fun of learning. Arnold (1970: 1) described physical education as that part of the educational process which 'enhances and harmonises the physical, intellectual, social and emotional aspects of an individual's personality, chiefly through direct physical activities'. It is this holistic, inclusive approach to physical education that has been at the heart of the planning of the book.

The book is organized into six chapters, each of which follows the series pattern through consideration of the child, the teacher and the context for learning. At the end of each chapter are questions for further consideration. The chapter topics are used to examine those key aspects of child development that underpin physical literacy and those factors which together integrate in the pursuit and achievement for children of becoming physically educated, through active teaching and active learning. One of the aims of the book is to provide primary practitioners with opportunities for reflecting on their current practice with a view to making whatever changes may be necessary, to raise standards. Another aim is to raise issues about provision and about finding ways to tackle the sometimes limited physical education provision in some schools and settings, capitalizing on partnerships and other creative ways of achieving sufficient time and quality teaching. There is intentional overlap between chapters, since PE is not a discrete discipline, but exists alongside and is integrated with other aspects of children's learning such as play, language and creativity. As not all teachers currently teach every aspect of physical education to the highest level, suggestions are made of ways to build on strengths and to address areas for further development.

Chapter 1 explores children's physical and motor development, including the ways in which development takes place from the top of the body downwards and from the centre of the body outwards. The analysis of ways in which movement is learnt focuses on gross and fine motor functioning, leading on to consideration of the several stages through which the learner progresses towards the acquisition of maturity in fundamental movement patterns. These themes lead into Chapter 2 on play. Throughout the period of growth and motor development, play is seen as of paramount importance, as a medium for learning through physical activity, as a natural medium of self-expression and as a creative function of human behaviour. Further development of some of the early themes leads on, in Chapter 3, to exploration of the relationship of language to physical literacy and creative activity. The final three chapters of the book turn to consideration of aspects of what it is to be physically educated. In Chapter 4, processes of observation of movement and development of effective feedback to enhance performance are analysed. Whereas play is spontaneous, is directed to no particular overall end and is an expression of uninhibited absorption (Arnold 1970: 2), physical education is directed, conforms to the application of the curriculum of the subject and requires deliberation and reflection on performance, knowledge and understanding. Chapter 5 discusses the subject of physical education, the various activities that are the components of this subject and the learning available, by means of effective teaching, through the delivery of a broad and balanced curriculum. Finally, in Chapter 6, active teaching and active learning are proposed as being central to the raising of standards in physical literacy and physical education for children. The whole book is illustrated with photographs of children and with examples of experience observed and reported by children and by teachers.

Three key questions that the book seeks to address are:

1 How can children achieve their entitlement to gain physical literacy and to become physically educated?
2 How can parents and teachers ensure that children's movement development and movement education are of the highest quality?
3 What are the most appropriate contexts for facilitating children's physicality?

1

Physical and motor development

These children are enjoying a controlled running game in which they show their skill.

Cameo 2

David and Cheryl (aged 6) are enjoying outdoor playtime, demonstrably revelling in their abilities and achievements as they chase around the area, stopping to catch their breath and then setting off again. When asked what they do best, David says that he is best at running really fast and Cheryl says that she is best at hopping and balancing on one foot. When asked what they like doing most, he says he likes football and she says she likes climbing, swinging and going down the slide in the adventure playground. In the classroom they both like working on the computer.

Cameo 3

David and Cheryl's teacher is looking at the physical development of the children in her class, in order to mentor the trainee teacher working with her. She notes the quite significant contrast in size between the tallest and the shortest child and is keen for her trainee to find out whether children of the same age are making similarly paced progress in gross and fine motor skills, regardless of their size. She is also interested to know whether the more advanced children in gross motor skills are further ahead in fine skills. Her trainee teacher, whose specialist subject is physical education, has drawn up an observation schedule and is observing the children during lessons and at play. He is surprised by what he sees and, over several weeks, records more significant differences than he was expecting to find, based on the books he has read which gave the averages for motor skill development of 6-year-old children.

Introduction

What is significant about the growth and physical development of David and Cheryl? How have they become so skilful at such a tender age and what accounts for the similarities and differences between them? In this chapter we explore aspects of children's growth, the development of motor competence, the achievement of mature movement patterns and the implications of these on moving to learn and learning to move.

The child

For the child, the early years are exciting times for growing, for changing shape and size and for looking forward to growing bigger. Emphasis on growth as a sign of maturation is often reinforced by parents, teachers and other adults, who compliment children on how big they are, how tall they are growing and how much they are growing up. Clothing provides further evidence of growth, such as when the coat 'that came right down to me' when it was first new for starting school soon became the too-short coat which was passed down to the younger child in the family. Such constant reminders are significant childhood measures of progress. A key benchmark in my own childhood was the long-awaited birthday each year, which was also the measuring day, to find out how much taller I had grown. To see the new mark on the height chart on the wall, and to know how much higher up this mark was than its predecessor, constituted an important part of celebrating that birthday.

Childhood is also an exciting time for gaining control of the body, for increasing in strength, speed, power, coordination and balance, for discovering what the body can do and for learning new skills. In Cameo 2, David and Cheryl are full of excitement, pleasure and confidence in all that they can do. Bearing in mind that they have gone around on legs for only about five years, it is not surprising that they have a real sense of achievement. As one child was heard to say after a physical education lesson in which games skills were being taught: 'I never knew I could catch a ball and now I can. I wonder if I'll be able to do something else that I can't do, next time'. Discoveries such as this are surely part of the child's birthright and, when celebrated, become landmarks in the adventure that is sometimes known as becoming physically literate. What can physical children expect from childhood, in achieving that physical literacy? They can expect both to learn how to move and to learn through moving to learn about the world around, about the self and about others. Since maturation alone will not account for the development of mature movement patterns, children can expect to be given opportunity to experience movement in a wide variety of contexts and environments and to receive instruction and encouragement and to have opportunity for practice.

If growth is defined as the process by which the child increases in size, weight, height and power, and physical development is defined as the process through which the child gains coordination, movement skills and abilities and becomes physically literate, what are the significant features of these processes for the physical child and the active teacher? First, it is undeniably the case that both growth and development take place in the same sequence in every normal child. Second, the pace at which growth

Figure 1.1   Motor development in infants
Source: Rathus (1988: 202)

and development take place is dependent on individual traits, environment and child-rearing practices. No two children grow and develop in exactly the same way and each child can look forward to a unique experience, not expecting to be exactly the same as anyone else and yet looking forward to achieving physical literacy. Thus, the 'norms' that feature in the literature illustrating rates of child development can be regarded only as examples of average developmental rates. For example, Figure 1.1 shows the invariant sequence of achieving locomotion, but the suggested ages at which each stage appears will vary from infant to infant.

Two processes are at work in determining movement development. These are known as cephalo-caudal development and proximo-distal development. Cephalo-caudal development is so named because it stems from the Greek word for 'head' which is 'cephale' and the Latin word for 'tail' which is 'cauda' from the head to the feet. This seems obvious since the top of the body, the head, is already well developed at birth, in order that the brain can fulfil its role in controlling all bodily functions. By contrast, the feet and legs are relatively undeveloped and of relatively little importance at this stage, since their functions are not required until later in life, when mobility and locomotion develop. Muscular development follows the same top-down sequence: control of the head is achieved prior to musculature to gain control of the shoulders. Once the infant can hold up the head unaided, the spinal muscles develop to enable the sitting position to be achieved, aided and then unaided. In the normal infant, activities like creeping and crawling continue the top-down development as the legs gain strength to assist in propelling the body along. This new-found leg strength contributes to the next developmental stage in which the child learns to stand with help and then without help. From there, aided walking leads to the taking of that all-important first step alone. This top-down development continues on into childhood and adulthood as the musculature to the ankles and feet strengthens and as the child gains experience in extending and flexing the ankles to gain more efficient mobility, locomotion and propulsion, in order to increase speed of travel, height of jump and efficiency in landing.

Research reported by Goddard Blythe (2000: 23) confirms that children who had difficulties in reading, writing and copying had learned to walk relatively late and many had not experienced the developmental stage of crawling on their tummies and on hands and knees. Such children tended to be later also in talking, riding a bicycle, catching a ball and in fine motor tasks such as are needed for dressing. They also found it harder to sit still, which is not surprising according to Goddard Blyth (2000: 23): 'the most advanced level of movement is the ability to stay totally still'.

Extending the ankles, often inaccurately referred to as 'pointing the toes', is an underdeveloped ability for many children. Lack of awareness of the ankle joint's facility to flex and extend can occur when insufficient attention is paid to cephalo-caudal development and to the development of the proprioceptive system. Proprioceptors in the muscles and joints enable us to be aware of the position of our limbs and body and to achieve accurate movement without having to monitor everything we do visually. Efficient proprioception also enables adjustments to be made to ensure that we keep our balance and adjust to our environment, for example, when walking on an uneven surface.

Proximo-distal development is the process whereby motor or movement control emerges from proximal (close to the body) to distal, further from the centre of the body. In infancy the distal parts of the body, namely the arms, hands and fingers, are relatively underdeveloped as their functions are not required until needed for body propulsion and manipulation. In this way the musculature to the shoulder girdle gains strength before that to the elbows, wrists, hands and finally to the fingers. Taking advantage of the early development of the musculature to the shoulders, the infant uses the whole arm to 'swipe' and bat at objects. Later both arms are used simultaneously to reach out towards objects, to grab a toy with both hands in the mid-line or centre of the body, using the muscles of both shoulders together to achieve greater efficiency. It is not until later that bilateral coordination develops, whereby the hands can be purposefully engaged in activities different from one another. Distinct lack of differentiation in the joints of the arms is evident for several months after birth and for several years in relation to the hands. Ability to use the hands and fingers efficiently develops much later. Indeed, we are not born with all the bones that we shall have in later life. For example, at birth the bones of the wrists are not yet differentiated. Proximo-distal development dictates that the wrist bones will separate and develop their own musculature over several years. This accounts for the gradual development of manipulative skills and for the process which enables the child to develop from the two-handed grabbing described above, to the single hand using a palmar grip and finally to the single hand using the pincer grip. The palmar or power grip can be seen when the whole hand is used for grasping, for example where the child folds all the fingers together around the tool to be grasped, enclosing it between the palm and the fingers, in a vertical position so that the tool is moved using the muscles of the shoulder and arm rather than the fingers. Because the distance of the movement from the source of that movement is so great, the resulting movements achieved are relatively large and uncontrolled.

By contrast, the pincer or precision grip requires differenti-

Figure 1.2 My rainbow by Jahneece (aged 3)

ation of activity between the fingers and thumb and considerable muscalature to the wrist, hand, fingers and thumb. Jahneece (aged 3) nicely shows the pincer grip as she holds her paint brush (Figure 1.2). This enables objects to be grasped, normally between the index finger and thumb, using the second finger as a guide.

In learning to write, this offers a more streamlined, near-horizontal position for the pencil and enables the other fingers and the side of the hand to assist in guiding and controlling the pencil. Also, because the source of the movement is the muscles of the fingers, it is possible to achieve smaller movements and therefore to produce smaller writing.

Although there are several normal and efficient deviations from this method of gripping the writing tool, the sequence of palmar to pincer grip is invariant.

If children are required to form legible letters and are given writing tasks before the developmental processes of bone differentiation and strengthening of the muscles to the wrist bones have adequately been achieved, the result can be frustration and inhibition in achievement. While these developments are taking place, children suffer from muscle fatigue during lengthy periods of writing, drawing and cutting activities. Children need short bursts of activity, with rests or contrasting activities in between, to enable the muscles to recover, to regain strength and then to be able to sustain the duration of ever-increasing work sessions.

While focusing on proximo-distal development and particularly the use of the hands, it may be interesting to look at the development of 'handedness' which emerges during early and middle childhood. The majority of the population is right-handed, with about 10 per cent only being left-handed. Handedness is normally well established by the age of 6 and children usually know left from right by the age of 7. It was often thought that left-handed children were more clumsy, but Tan (1985, cited in Owens 1993: 185) reports that it was the children who were lacking any hand preference who scored significantly lower in motor skill tests. Tan suggests: 'the lack of hand preference may serve as a marker indicating children who need special assistance with the development of motor skills to improve their motor coordination' (Owens 1993: 123). Establishing movement patterns and particularly the determination of the dominant hand is due to the particular relationship between brain and the body, in that the right and left sides of the body are controlled by the opposite side of the brain. Thus the right side of the body is controlled by the left side of the brain and the left side of the body by the right side of the brain.

Determining which hand will be more responsible for holding things steady and controlling their weight, and which hand takes on the fiddly tasks, is the basis for developing handedness. Prior to achieving bilateral coordination, children appear not to cross the mid-line to pick up objects, for example. If the object is on the right side of the body, the right hand would be used and similarly, left for objects on the left side. Once hand preference for writing is established, the dominant hand and foot are often the same. However, there are normal exceptions. For example, some children write with the right hand and prefer to kick with the left foot (Rathus 1988: 208). For children a very important aspect of cephalo-caudal and proximo-distal development is the development of hand and foot dominance. Control of hands and feet enable the child to be successful, to be able to learn new skills,

Figure 1.3 Brett (aged 4) carefully fixes legs on to his monster

to enhance the old and to increase in self-confidence and self-esteem among peers.

In Figure 1.3, Brett (aged 4) coordinates his hands both to hold the monster with one hand and to fix on a leg with the other. This is a good example of lateralization whereby the two limbs can be controlled while engaging in different tasks. Using movement as a means of learning about the world is a key developmental element for the normal child. Movement is the main medium of exploration for the infant, by using the sense-orientated activity of the eyes, ears, touch, taste to elicit movement and to respond actively to stimuli. For example, the sound of a rattle elicits a turning of the head towards the sound, the sight of the rattle elicits a reaching out to grasp the rattle and to discover the properties of the rattle if it is then drawn towards, and put into, the mouth. This ability is known as sensori-motor activity. For the Key Stage 2 child (aged 7–11 years), that early experimentation in movement underpins later experiences, such as, for example, picking up and feeling the texture of a range of materials, in order to test their durability during a science investigation.

In normal child development the ability to move about, to roll over, crawl and walk, to grasp, hold and release objects, is central. It is through movement also that a child can express moods and feelings, such as stamping and writhing in anger, or waving and hugging as expressions of joy and love. Movement is also used to engage in creative play, to trot as a horse or to sway like a tree. Through their own voluntary actions children acquire experiences that enable them to interpret their ever-expanding world and to learn about the properties both of objects and their immediate environment. By means of repetition of actions, they both refine and improve efficiency and mastery of actions and discover the consistency and inconsistency of the environments in which they move. Increased opportunities for activities such as these are particularly important for children who have to overcome dyspraxia, or other problems of delayed movement development in early childhood. Providing appropriate learning support is vital for children who have motor skill difficulties, such as managing to eat with a spoon, running with coordination, riding a bike or writing. For example, a child might be deemed as having failed to know a concept, such as the shape of a cube in maths, due to an inability to engage skilfully and efficiently in the practical construction of that shape which involves accurate management of measuring, cutting and sticking tools. This may be due to delayed hand–eye coordination or to insufficient time for development or regular practice of relevant gross and fine motor skills, to enable them to acquire the strength, skill and confidence necessary to undertake the original task. While the majority of children achieve a wide range of ontogenetic skills early in life, it falls to the teacher to provide each child with appropriate progressions and to take account of the differing abilities and interests of boys and girls when planning for play and movement education.

In normal development the multitude of early experiences forms the basis for, and gives nourishment to, the development in the older child of intellectual activity. The child begins to increase conceptual powers and to engage in logical thought and abstraction. Indeed movement is a key factor underpinning all other areas of learning. Much evidence of this is seen in classrooms and other settings where young children are educated and cared for. Contexts for this learning, including indoor and outdoor environments that offer clear and often large space, allow for freedom of movement and for the encouragement of gross and fine motor skill development, which will be discussed later. The role of the teacher in enabling children to develop to their full potential follows now.

The teacher

For the teacher of young children and those in Key Stages 1 and 2 (aged 5–11 years), knowledge and understanding of patterns of growth, physical and motor development are central to the provision of appropriate learning experiences and environments for their school life and education. Pre-school and primary school teaching involves extensive application of knowledge of motor behaviour and motor development. Motor behaviour is the product of growth and development and describes observable changes in movement ability and where motor development refers to the emerging abilities and learned skills that enable the child to work towards achieving full movement potential.

Goddard Blythe (2000: 23) reports on tests for readiness to learn to write carried out in the former Czechoslovakia:

- draw a circle in both a clockwise and an anti-clockwise direction
- touch the left ear with the right hand and the right foot with the left hand.

These simple motor abilities were found to confirm children's readiness to form letters and to work from the left to the right side of the page when writing.

'Gross' and 'fine' motor functioning correspond to cephalo-caudal and proximo-distal development in the way that they emerge in the maturing infant. 'Gross' or large muscle activity develops prior to 'fine' or small muscle movement, thus enabling the child to achieve body stability and to move the legs and arms as whole units, before muscular differentiation takes place to enable the smaller muscles to develop and control separate parts of the limbs and their finer movements.

Rathus (1988) proposed examples of stages of development of motor abilities in children, along with suggested ages around which these skills might be seen to develop (Table 1.1).

The trainee teacher in Cameo 3 found wide variations in the performance of these activities among the children he observed.

Table 1.1   Stages of motor development in children

Gross motor development

Age 3	stand on one foot, walk upstairs with alternating feet, jump from step, kick a large ball, hop two or three times
Age 4	run smoothly, throw a ball overarm, pedal a tricycle, gallop, skip (step, hop) using one foot, hop along and on the spot, five or six times
Age 5	walk in a straight line, walk downstairs with alternating feet, catch a bounced ball, march in rhythm, walk on a balance beam, jump along about 1 metre, jump for height about 30 cm
Age 6	hop, jump, climb, throw a ball using wrist and fingers, skip with alternate feet, gallop (step and leap, same foot leading), skip
Age 7	pedal a bicycle, hit a ball with a bat from a T
Age 8	good body balance, skill 'hungry'
Age 9	engage in vigorous activity, sports and games
Age 10	balance on one foot for 15 seconds, catch a small ball thrown at speed

Fine motor development

Age 3	pick up blocks, place shapes in holes, turn pages of a book, unbutton clothes, hold cup in one hand
Age 4–5	hold pencil with pincer grip, copy a square accurately, colour within lines
Age 6–7	tie shoelaces, hold pencil with fingertips
Age 8–9	space words when writing, write and print accurately, sew and knit, good hand–eye coordination

Source: Adapted from Rathus (1988: 205)

Not only were there significant differences in the ways in which children performed the tasks indicated within the age band, but also some children were capable of achieving tasks allocated to older age groups. Gross motor skills involve both mobility and balance. In the young child, mobility develops first, followed by the development of musculature to control stability. When teaching hopping, you may notice that the immature 'hopper' tends to hop along, rather than hopping on the spot, since the latter requires greater stability to balance over the hopping foot, while taking off from and landing on to the same foot. Many motor behaviours are known as phylogenetic because they emerge naturally as the normal child matures. Others are ontogenetic, that is, they are influenced by learning and the environment. Early abilities such as reaching, grasping, walking and running are examples of phylogenetic skills, while cycling, swimming and roller-blading are examples of ontogenetic skills. Maturation, prior experience and practice all contribute to the achievement of competence, efficiency and accuracy of each skill and lead to the 'moment of readiness' to acquire a new skill.

Skills can be seen to emerge and develop towards maturity in what Gallahue (1989) has defined broadly in three stages (Table 1.2). The first stumbling and often uncoordinated attempts constitute the *initial stage*. These lead into the *elementary stage* and, when the skill is streamlined, efficient and well coordinated, the *mature stage* is finally achieved.

The children in Cameo 1 have all achieved a mature running pattern, yet each has a unique style and the range of efficiency and speed is quite considerable. All of these children are eager to be taught now, how to run faster. As teachers, in addition to gaining knowledge and understanding of the stages of development of all fundamental motor skills, we are always preparing children for more complex tasks. We need to be able to assess the 'moment of readiness' for a new piece of learning, while also enabling each child to take full advantage of their current ability and level of maturation, with poised anticipation, ready to take on the next challenge. Assessing when to present that next progression is an ongoing target for the teacher.

How often have we, as adults, run along holding the saddle of a beginner bike rider, trying to decide just how much longer it will take before we can let go? Judging the moment of readiness to let go, or to remove the stabilizer wheels, is quite a skill and Richard (aged 4) has already convinced his parents that he is ready (Figure 1.4)! Lack of coordination and precision in the movement of young children is due partly to the fact that the nerve paths which conduct impulses from the brain to the various parts of the body are not 'isolated'. The young child's reactions therefore involve the whole body in the early stages of both gross and fine motor skill developments. For example, in throwing a ball, the action of the throwing hand is often mirrored by the other hand. The process whereby neural mechanisms work together to allow

Table 1.2   Developmental sequence in running

A *Initial stage*
    1 Short, limited leg swing.
    2 Stiff, uneven stride.
    3 No observable flight phase.
    4 Incomplete extension of support leg.
    5 Stiff, short swing with varying degrees of elbow flexion.
    6 Arms tend to swing outward horizontally.
    7 Swinging leg rotates outward from hip.
    8 Swinging foot toes outward.
    9 Wide base of support.

B *Elementary stage*
    1 Increase in length of stride, arm swing and speed.
    2 Limited but observable flight phase.
    3 More complete extension of support leg at takeoff.
    4 Arm swing increases.
    5 Horizontal arm swing reduced on backswing.
    6 Swinging foot crosses mid-line at height of recovery to rear.

C *Mature stage*
    1 Stride length at maximum; stride speed fast.
    2 Definite flight phase.
    3 Complete extension of support leg.
    4 Recovery thigh parallel to ground.
    5 Arms swing vertically in opposition to legs.
    6 Arms bent at approximate right angles.
    7 Minimal rotary action of recovery leg and foot.

Source: Gallahue (1989: 238)

opposing muscle groups to work in a coordinated way is known as 'integration'. When integration is achieved, the muscles on each side of a joint together cooperate to facilitate coordinated movement. For example, to bend the elbow, the muscles crossing the back of the elbow over the 'funny bone' need to extend and the 'strong man' muscles crossing the front of the elbow need to contract and as they shorten they bring the forearm towards the upper arm, to bend the arm.

Throughout the growing period, the child continually and imperceptibly increases ability to control the body and the limbs and to develop precision and fluency of movement. Children's

Figure 1.4   Richard (aged 4) rides his bicycle with confidence

muscles grow considerably during the school years, not by add-ing muscle fibre, but through training of the muscles supplied at birth. Because children's muscles contain a greater percentage of water than those of adults, they tire more quickly and children must change position more frequently than their elders. This is why when we observe young children playing, even in seden-tary activities, they shift position, from sitting to standing to lying and to all stages in between, seemingly without disturbing their concentration on that activity. This natural and seemingly constant shifting satisfies the need to provide renewed stimula-tion to the muscles and to avoid muscle fatigue. This physiologi-cal fact was not always applied by curriculum developers. For example, a set of early learning goals for pre-school/pre-Key Stage 1 children (produced in 1999) targeted the ability to sit still as one of the necessary achievements for children aged 3–4, alongside the ability to count to 10 and to recognize and repeat stories. However, as Goddard Blythe (2000) reminds us: 'The most advanced level of movement is the ability to stay totally still'. To achieve stillness requires all the muscles controlling the postural systems as well as the mechanisms that control balance, to coordinate and work together. Children who are unable to sit still or pay attention are in need of more time for physical activities. In this way they will not only gain control of the involuntary movements that impede their ability to keep still but also increase their vocabulary of controlled, voluntary actions.

Lack of coordination and lack of precision in movement are hallmarks of very young children as they use the whole body for each activity. For example, children who have just started to walk usually stop by sitting down, rather than coming to a standstill balanced over the feet, as would older children. Young children when throwing a ball with one hand replicate that action with the other hand at the same time, being unable to differentiate the activities of the body. This is due to the fact that nerve pathways from the brain to the muscles are not yet 'embedded'. This embedding of nerve paths can significantly be assisted, and even hastened, through repetition and practice. Hence the importance for teachers of providing plenty of gross motor play and physical education.

The organization of movement around the mid-line of the body is vital for normal physical development. Much early movement learning takes place to develop control around the mid-line. For example, the infant brings the arms towards the mid-line to grasp a rattle and in early catching of a beanbag or ball we encourage the child to hold the hands together in the centre of the body (Figure 1.5).

The mid-line of the body is also the focal point for establishing upright posture. In learning to sit or to stand, the infant develops stability mechanisms centrally in order to balance in the vertical position on the bottom and later on the feet. Once the trunk can be stabilized with control, for example in the sitting position, the child can focus on performing other tasks, such as working out how the hands can operate separately, rather than together to achieve bilateral coordination. This opens up a whole new set of learning experiences, such as holding a drum steady with one hand while beating on it with the other, or holding a piece of Plasticine with one hand while cutting it to size with the other hand.

There are two types of muscles that work together to enable

Figure 1.5 Joshua (aged 7) catching a ball at the mid-line

the limbs to move and to facilitate upright posture and mobility. These are the extensor or stretching muscles and the flexor or bending muscles. In infancy the flexor muscles predominate, as observed when the child reverts to the foetal position with the arms and legs drawn in, bent and close to the body. However, by the age of 6 and again around the age of 11, the extensor muscles dominate and the child seems to need to and enjoys stretching out, reclining at length in chairs, lying stretched, full length, on the floor. How often has the teacher reminded children aged 6 and 11 to sit up at their desks, or on the carpet, or to sit cross-legged on the hall floor during assembly? How much are we aware that this runs counter to most children's natural prefer-ence for, and need to, stretch out? Another important aspect for teachers is to enable children to proceed from the ability to per-form skills as a result of thinking through the activity, then doing it, to performing that skill automatically. This depends on motor planning or praxis and includes conceiving, planning and execut-

Table 1.3   Increases in jumping

Activity	Age 6	Age 12
Vertical jump	10 cm	35 cm
Standing long jump	1 metre	1 metre 70 cm

Source: Cratty (1986: 35)

Table 1.4   Motor skill achievements

Activity	Age 6	Age 12
Speed of throw by a boy	11.7 metres per second	23.4 metres per second
Speed of throw by a girl	8.7 metres per second	16.8 metres per second
Speed of kick by a boy	6.3 metres per second	10.2 metres per second
Speed of kick by a girl	3.9 metres per second	7.8 metres per second

Source: Cratty (1986: 36)

ing the task. Efficient motor planning also depends on sufficiently developed cognitive abilities. Cratty (1986) looked at the relative achievements of children in a range of automatic motor skills and he recorded the average increase in distance/speed at age 6 and at age 12, in these skills. For example, at age 6, running speed was 3.66 m per second on average and by age 12 this had increased to over 5.49 m per second. Increases in jumping were found to be as shown in Table 1.3.

Cratty (1986) also found that there were significant differences in average achievement between girls and boys at both age 6 and at age 12, as shown in Table 1.4.

Skills such as hopscotch improve steadily from first achievement at the age of about 7, but level off at about the age of 9. Sarah (aged 5) is proficient in the foot pattern and locomotion of hopscotch (Figure 1.6). However, one indication that she has not achieved the mature stage is that her tongue is poking from her mouth and her hands are held awkwardly. Her whole body is not yet integrated in the activity. By contrast 11-year-old Emily's whole body and limbs are in perfect rhythm as she hops and jumps high and speedily from end to end of the game (Figure 1.7).

Figure 1.6 Sarah (aged 5) playing hopscotch

The ability to balance is fully developed in most children by the age of 9, with girls usually achieving more refined balance skill than boys. Changes in gross motor skills during middle childhood are quite sufficiently significant to require detailed attention when planning the environment for the child's day in school, to ensure opportunities for gross and fine motor activity both freely and through planned and structured teaching. Understanding the potential range of abilities and differences between children provide the teacher with useful benchmarks. Through assessing the relative development of the children they teach at various stages, teachers can then provide appropriate environments, tasks and time for both classroom-based learning and for appropriate physical education learning experience for each child.

Figure 1.7   Emily (aged 11) playing hopscotch

The context

Providing settings, time, resources and appropriate opportunities for young children to achieve maximum motor competence in gross and fine skills is an interesting challenge for the teacher. This is particularly so in the new millennium, in countries such as England, where trends towards knowledge-based rather than experience-based education seem to have been prevalent. Teacher training centres could be the vehicle for imparting the knowledge base for physical literacy, for defining progressions in the development of children's mature movement patterns and for providing training in observation and diagnostic assessment of movement. They could also structure and set up programmes in partnership with schools, for more effective teaching of physical education. The school system could provide regular and frequent opportunities for children to participate in appropriate physical activity, through play, taught sessions and extra-curricular activity. Where teachers accurately assess the level of motor skill of each child, they also plan for and provide appropriate tasks in the classroom, such that no child is hindered from learning an academic skill or concept, on account of an underdeveloped motor skill. Similarly, every child can be exposed to the physical tasks that will best develop optimum physical literacy and be continually challenged, as each successive 'moment of readiness' is attained and surpassed by the next.

'Not to let children move about is a sure way to tire them out' (Noren-Bjorn 1997: 31), since the ability to move around and to manipulate objects is central to normal development.

Through their own actions, children acquire experience of the causal connections that govern the physical world. Later, when they gradually begin to increase their conceptual powers and to engage in logical thought and abstraction, the multitude of early experiences forms the basis for, and gives nourishment to, this

Figure 1.8 Hadid (aged 5) on his favourite tricycle

intellectual activity (Noren-Bjorn 1982: 39). Assessing children's stages of development and experience provides the basis for curriculum planning in order to meet the needs of those children.

Physical and motor development is greatly enhanced by exposure to ample spaces and large toys, which provide excellent opportunities for the development of gross motor skills. Young children need a large area to turn a corner while running, or in steering pedal cars, tricycles or scooters, for example (Figure 1.8).

Many nursery and primary school indoor and outdoor environments are now designed to provide for enhancement of both gross and fine motor skills. Indoor settings include sand, as well as water play, areas for construction, manipulations and body awareness, all of which can help to stimulate physical and motor development. Boorman (1998: 12) suggests ways of catering for the range of essential skill development areas for children in the foundation stage (age 3–5 years: see Table 1.5).

Boorman (1998) also suggests types of equipment and resources that offer versatility and excitement as well as challenging physical activity (Table 1.6).

Table 1.5 Essential skill developments

- Mobility skills: running, jumping, hopping, crawling
- Agility skills: stretching, balancing, twisting, climbing, dancing
- Construction skills: building, assembling, lifting, carrying, placing and arranging objects
- Communication skills: gesture, non-verbal communication, expression
- Fine motor manipulative skills: appropriate handling of tools, instruments and malleable materials
- Projection skills: grasping, releasing, rolling, throwing, aiming, kicking
- Body awareness: sensing what it feels like to be upside-down
- Spatial awareness: under, through, at the side of, looking from different perspectives
- Temporal awareness: judging speed, moving slowly
- Directional awareness: sideways, backwards, forwards, with awareness of others

Source: Boorman (1998: 12)

Table 1.6 Equipment and resources for early learning

- Simple versatile materials: crates, tyres, logs, earth, sand, planks
- Resources for children to paint or write on a large scale: such as huge paint brushes and water, or large pieces of chalk
- Varied opportunities for children to push, pull and transport objects of varying sizes and weights
- Playground road markings and traffic signs to encourage controlled steering and awareness of direction
- Shelter and props to encourage children's imaginative play
- Covers, blankets or tents to stimulate imaginative and physical play
- Patches of ground and sand for digging
- Opportunities for playing hide and seek and following treasure trails

---

Source: Boorman (1998: 13)

Summary

Achievement of the range or skill developments suggested by Boorman (1998) along with exposure to, and experience of, the equipment and resources that she recommends can do much to ensure children's motor competence. Moving to learn and learning to move are key to the child's overall development and time given to practising physical activities cannot be underestimated or compromised.

In the next chapter, consideration is given to play and to the experiences and expertise that the physical child can gain through well-provisioned play opportunities, with knowledgeable teachers and carers offering appropriate intervention to enhance learning.

Questions to ask

1 How can you provide more opportunities for children to improve their gross and fine motor functioning?
2 What more do you need to know in order to analyse and enhance children's physical literacy as they seek to achieve mature movement patterns?
3 How can you improve the environment to provide enhanced opportunities for motor development?
4 Are there other resources that you could provide to increase the pace or range of children's skill acquisition?

2

Play

Cameo 1

In their nursery class David and Emma are busy dressing up in space-suits, getting ready for blast off and eager to walk on the moon, while Sarah and Hadid are enthusiastically pedalling and skilfully steering trikes around the circuitous pathways on the playground.

Cameo 2

Year 6 pupils (aged 10–11 years) in their primary school can opt to be trained as play leaders. Their role is to facilitate the play both of younger children from the age of 3 and with their peers and to stimulate physical play for all children during the school breaktimes. The pupil play leaders distribute and collect in play equipment and play with younger children at morning break and additionally organize teams and referee friendly mini-matches for older children during the lunch break. Gale says: 'I enjoy being a play leader because I like helping younger children'. Peter says: 'I know that football, basketball, short tennis and other games like hoops, diabolo, skipping and wall games help to keep you healthy, keep you warm in cold weather and you get better at PE by practising at break'.

Introduction

In this chapter play is regarded as learning with the body. Play is seen as a means of enabling children to engage in motor skill activities, to acquire mature movement patterns in fundamental motor skills, to explore a range of environments, to use physical play to enhance the development of language, social and cognitive development and to indulge in exercise as a means in itself. For young children, play is the child's main business of life (Lee 1984: 34). Play and work are not necessarily differentiated, particularly when the activities are engrossing and pleasurable. This idea is corroborated in the *Early Learning Goals* (Qualifications and Curriculum Authority (QCA) 1999a: 4), which state: 'They [children] do not make a distinction between play and work and neither should practitioners'.

> Play is an extremely important human activity; it is a basis for culture. Play is not only a primary biological function, but the primary function for man. Play is a process by which a child develops mature understanding; it is an exploration of one's self in relation to the world; it is a process of accepting oneself.
>
> (Saach 1988: 27)

In young children this lack of distinction between play and work can be seen when children work on the computer, share stories, paint or practise writing. Play is the centre of life. If there is a log to be climbed or jumped on to, the child will climb or jump on. If another child comes along and gets on, they may try to pass each other, or to push one another off, to go along together, or to make up a rhythm together of jumping on, off, or over. It is as if the act of jumping on to the log is a way of leaping away from the ordinary, to break away from the norm, to share another experience with someone else. 'Children are geniuses at play and should be given environments in which they can display this genius' (Mitsuru 1992: 78). The children in Cameo 1 not only demonstrated their genius ability, but also had an excellent environment in which to play. Saach suggests that play and culture are so fundamentally interrelated that the play and learning of children are absolutes for human survival, whereby children explore themselves in relation to the world, they engage in a process of self-development, as they develop mature understanding. It is this learning process that is fundamental to human survival.

Much of the literature on play seems to focus on the intellectual, cognitive, emotional and social aspects of children's development, with little reference to the means by which children play, namely their physical selves. The perspective of this chapter is about the contributions that play can make in children's physical development, since physical play involves both gross motor, large muscle development and fine motor, small muscle development, as well as perceptual motor development. Play areas and play teaching for physical development should take account of the following learning opportunities for children. Play areas should include opportunities for the strengthening of physical skills by using large and small muscle groups:

- to develop motor, rhythmic and kinaesthetic sense
- to develop dexterity and skill in manipulating objects
- to develop hand–eye and foot–eye coordination
- to develop body and spatial awareness, as well as awareness of physical capabilities and limitations.

Play provision should take account of play limitations as well as capabilities, the power of play in facilitating motor skill acquisition and in providing endless opportunities for practice, repetition and refinement of physical skills. The importance of active play as a medium for exercise, and as an essential stimulant to healthy growth and development, will also be considered. The contributions of physical play to the development of drawing, language, cognitive and social development, to the development of imaginative play and to early explorations of creativity will be discussed. Examples are drawn from the many physical activities that children engage in when they play freely and in guided situations. The chapter is structured to include first of all, contexts for play, then the child at play and finally the role of the teacher in developing children's play.

Contexts of play

Recorded theories of play date back to Plato, whose laws cited, for example, the provision of miniature tools to 3 year olds who would later become builders, and the distribution of apples to children to aid the learning of arithmetic. More recent educationists, including Pestalozzi and Froebel, recognized the contribution of play to learning, incorporating children's natural interests and stages of development in their educational planning. Whereas classical theorists seemed to find a single function for play, it is now widely accepted that play consists of a great diversity of activities that serve many purposes and fulfil several different needs. Play is usually both an earnest and an enjoyable activity. Piaget divided child development into various stages, from the reflexive responses of the new-born, through the sensori-motor stage in infancy, through the constructive then symbolic play stages, leading to the eventual achievement of logical adult thinking, each with its own characteristic form of play. Post-Piagetian researchers have both built from his work and moved on from some of his more rigid analyses.

Bruce (1991) proposes four main types of play: functional play, constructive play, rule-governed play and socio-dynamic play. Through functional play, children engage in natural developmental activities, they learn about their capabilities, they explore sensori-motor activity, they repeat, refine, practise and remember what they enjoy doing and begin to develop their movement memory. They also extend their movement vocabulary for future recall and use in a variety of contexts. Activities such as walking, rolling over, climbing up and down, jumping and hopping can be seen as examples of functional play.

Constructive play takes over when children begin to organize activity according to their own plan, incorporating materials and objects into their play. Building sand-castles, making a click-lix model or marking out a circuit for toy cars are examples of constructive play. Other characteristics of constructive play are that something is left behind and there is an obvious sense of enjoyment in the activity of constructing (Figure 2.1).

Rule-governed play can broadly be located in one of two categories, physical games, usually involving gross motor activity, and table games, more often involving fine motor activity. For this type of play to be successful, children must have reached the stage of being able to conform to rules and to have agreed to play according to those rules.

Socio-dynamic play often involves drama in which children express their growing awareness of their social setting. This develops from an early age in parallel to other play behaviours. The child acts out social interaction and in so doing, can experience human relationships actively by means of symbolic representation.

Play structures such as climbing frames and adventure playgrounds provide great opportunities for all kinds of developmental play. From his research into the best designs for children's play environments and structure, Mitsuru (1992: 13) suggests that when children are using play structures there are three stages in

Figure 2.1 How many bricks in this tower?

the development of their play. The first of these is 'functional play', when children first experience a play structure they tend to use it for the purpose for which it was designed. For example, they will climb up the steps to sit at the top of a slide and slide down in the sitting position.

After repeating this activity, many children move on to the second stage known as the stage of 'technical' play. They begin to explore the potential of that structure for inventing new ways of moving and new activities to try. For example, they go down the slide head first, or start at the bottom and push and pull up the slide, to get to the top, instead of taking the easy way up by climbing the steps. The technical stage enables children to continue to have fun, through devising their own ways of exploring ideas and finding out new possibilities of that play structure.

The third stage, in which children play games involving the play structure, but not in the way intended, such that the play structure is merely the setting for play, is known as the stage of 'social' play. For example, the slide is used as part of a game of tag between two or more children, or the slide is used as a barrier between the catcher and the rest. The slide has now become part of the setting for another game and the children's focus is on playing tag. Ideally, play structures should lend themselves to all three stages, in keeping with the stages of development of children's play, namely functional, technical and social. Children will then acquire fundamental motor skills, improve on them and use them to play even more complex games.

Each of these types of play provide for physical development needs and for the flourishing of gross and fine motor skill and coordination. The variety of provision of structured environments such as playgrounds or water areas, or unstructured settings and environments, can greatly enhance the range and quality of physical play, for children in their early years of schooling and right through the primary school years. Physical play activities include structured games such as hopscotch and football; non-structured play such as climbing, swinging and sliding; and perceptual and fine motor activities, such as handicrafts and building a tree house. A good play space leads children to play freely and without restriction. Mitsuru (1992: 86) proposed that 'a child's play environment consists of four elements; a place to play, time to play, others to play with and what they actually do'. All four elements are indispensable and, at the same time, are mutually interrelated in a complex web.

The quality of each of these elements greatly influences the quality of the play. For example, Mitsuru suggests that a 12-year-old child should have four to five hours per day of outdoor play, in 1 to 2 hectares of space, with four to ten playmates, engaging in a variety of sports and games, with very active periods interspersed with times for recovery. While this may seem unrealistic, he also suggested a number of helpful requirements for the provision of satisfactory space and equipment for physical play. First, there must be sufficient space for a clear flow of movement, so that the separate play provisions, such as a climbing net, bridge and swinging tyre, must also be capable of becoming one big activity area. Second, the whole area and the activities within it must be safe yet challenging, and should provide for endless

Figure 2.2 I've reached the top to hoist the flag

variety of activity. Third, there must be many routes through the area, with shortcuts and bypasses. Fourth, to allow for an endless choice of journeys there must be symbolic high places, where children can feel that they have scaled the heights (Figure 2.2).

A fifth requirement is the provision of places to experience dizziness, allowing children to throw themselves off play structures and land safely. There must also be places in which to hide. Finally, there need to be large and small gathering places and the whole environment must be open with a variety of access places, so that the area is 'porous'.

For older children the larger the circulation space the better, allowing for speedy activity for chasing and for mastering obstacles. Since play is enhanced when there is challenge, the provision of contrasting environments is important. There need to be

Figure 2.3 A neighbourhood play area

high and low places, soft and hard places, wide open spaces as well as narrow, constricting spaces, dark and light, bright places and shady places. Play structures must also be pleasing to the eye, attractive in design, well maintained and located in a pleasant setting (Figure 2.3).

Mitsuru (1992: 15) found that a variety of game-types that were generated on play structures could be categorized broadly as competition, chase games and fighting. Competition games might involve one child trying to reach an end point before another, such as climbing up the sides of a play structure, or racing down a double slide and climbing back up again. Chase games include a variety of tag games, using the many routes over, under, around, along and through play structures and games such as 'cops and robbers'. Such games involve going at speed and they allow for dizziness experiences such as sliding, spinning and jumping. Imitation games are those in which children often use both gross and fine motor skills as they pretend to be shopping, housekeeping, playing school, or navigating a ship or space craft, for example. A multifunction play area, satisfying the requirements listed above, can help to generate rich play activities and give opportunity for children to invent new games. Ideal playscapes might include an open or wooded and hilly grass space, for sitting, rolling down or sledging in winter, a sand area, a roller-blading area with ramp, play structures, a wall as a rebound surface and an asphalt area for ball play, marked with grids and play shapes. Ideally, these would be interrelated to enable children of different ages to mingle and play at the same time, with platforms for pausing and resting connected to activity areas that encourage activity and speed. In Ottawa in Canada, a network of bike paths have been constructed to facilitate safe, off-the-road biking for children as well as adults, who also use them for walking and jogging. In Britain, alternative outdoor play places can include the street, the garden, the beach and the countryside. Great indoor play places for developing gross motor skills include ball baths, bouncy castles, swimming pools and sports halls.

The context of play also encompasses the range of equipment that can support children's play. Noren-Bjorn (1997) provided categories of equipment, where equipment for exercise is subdivided into two categories: simple functions and combined functions. Under simple function she included balancing equipment, beams, walls and natural areas such as kerbs, fences and walls, climbing frames, with rope ladders, nets and (where possible) trees. Noren-Bjorn noted that children mostly choose daring places to balance, rather than the standard balance beam provided on a playground, unless it is suspended. Walls marked for ball play with feet, hands, bats, sticks and rackets would also be in this category. Equipment for exercise combined with sensory experiences of speed, spinning and dizziness include swings and (traditional and tyre) slides, which are probably the most used item for play and experiments with speed, gravity, friction and sound. Slides give experience of height and a shifting perspective. Slides can be used to go down by sliding down on the seat, front or back, head first, feet first, seat on material, alone and in twos or rows. They are also great for trying to climb back up.

Carousel, seesaw, suspension bridge, suspended beam or log and rocking horse offer a range of unstable experiences. The rocking horse can also be used for climbing on and off, as much as for rocking and children can be seen standing on a rocking horse practising circus tricks. For older children aerial ropeways, skateboarding ramps or any other assault course type of equipment which resembles media games, such as *It's a Knockout*, provide excellent playful, motor development challenges.

Toys can be both vehicles for the growth of normal abilities and tools for movement development and instruments for play. Activities with toys involve a variety of kinds of learning, including exploration, mastery and imagination. In the first few years they are largely tools for development, as children learn the basic manual and manipulative skills. From the age of 2 or 3, the play function becomes dominant and the toys themselves become increasingly important, including the way they are packaged and presented. By the age of 4 or 5, imaginary roles are given to toys and children often use them to fulfil more than one function. For example, a ball can be at one time a cannon-ball and at another a kangaroo, bouncing away. From age 6–8 years, children's toys, hobbies, games and sports increasingly play a role in shaping their concept of themselves and also have a part to play in affecting their developing abilities. Contexts of play including environments, structures, activities, games and toys, both indoors and outdoors, provide the physical child with a rich kaleidoscope of opportunities for both motor development and for using movement to learn about the world.

The child

In the infant, sensori-motor play develops increasing ability to organize and coordinate sensations with physical movements and actions as in, for example, looking at the hands, using the hands to touch the face and putting the hands into the mouth. As children grow, time devoted to playing physically is time well spent, not just for cardiovascular benefit, but also in using and strengthening the skeleto-muscular system and in developing body and spatial awareness and psychomotor competency. Opportunities for repetition and practice are seen as vital contributors in establishing movement patterns and in helping to increase the vocabulary of movement and skills needed to explore, discover and extend into new spheres of learning and experience. Physically active play contributes to exercising the body, which in turn promotes healthy development of the circulatory and digestive systems and may be seen as setting down a very early marker for the promotion of an active lifestyle in later years.

One of the great gifts of life is to know how to play (Slade

1995). Play may be calm or active, sometimes violently so. Slade (1995) divided play into two parts, which he called projected play and personal play. The distinction is of considerable importance. In projected play the body is mostly still, the person is sitting, lying, squatting or kneeling and the idea is projected into, on to or around objects outside them. Thus play with sand, string, stones, toys, dolls, writing and drawing, all come under this heading. Personal play, by contrast, involves the whole person. The person gets up and moves and takes full responsibility for the action. No longer does the toy live the life for you, you are up and doing it yourself. Thus running, dancing, acting, swimming and active sports of all kinds come under this heading. In personal play, once the child can move about without much risk of getting hurt, there is a new joy of discovery and freedom. The child can make journeys by crawling slowly, then quickly, then walking forwards, backwards, around, climbing under and over obstacles and, when more experienced, travelling by hopper, tricycle, scooter, roller-blades or skateboard.

Another form of play, well documented in the literature, is 'rough and tumble' play, which emerges at around 4 years, when children have mastered basic gross motor skills and try out these skills in fun with other children. Rough and tumble play involves running, jumping, chasing and fleeing, all carried out with a smile.

Learning to move and moving to learn have already been highlighted as key underpinning activities for the physical child and where better to discover about this learning than through play?

Running as fast as you can, falling over, getting up and running as fast as you can again is a source of considerable pride and accomplishment for the 3-year-old child, who no longer has to make an effort just to stay upright and who shows sheer delight in hopping along and jumping, in scribbling and building a tower with bricks. It has been found that 3-year-old children have the highest activity level of any age in the human life-span. They fidget when they watch television or listen to a story, or sit at the table to eat. They continue to move around even when asleep. To satisfy this need for movement and to encourage the development of the large muscles of the arms and legs, children need lots of exercise every day. Exercise has the added advantage of stimulating the development of the nervous system. The process whereby the nerve cells are covered and insulated with a layer of fat cells is known as myelination. This process has the effect of increasing the speed of information travelling through the nervous system. Myelination in relation to hand–eye coordination is not complete until around 4 years of age. The child is then at the moment of readiness for the acquisition of a wide range of skills, particularly the manipulative range of games skills. By the age of 4, children become more adventurous in their play, while still enjoying all their 3-year-old achievements. Now they display their athletic powers, they explore climbing frames, ride a bike and other play structures and enjoy wheeled toys such as tricycles and bikes with stabilizers. Physical play provides children with opportunities to acquire mature movement patterns, to increase movement vocabulary, to explore the environment, to indulge in exercise and to achieve psychomotor competence.

Table 2.1 lists some activities that promote movement development through play.

Equipment provides many starting points for children's play activities by enticing children into playing and by extending the range of possibilities. Fixed equipment which is static, such as slides and climbing frames, and moving equipment, such as, swings, tyre swings and suspended bridge, offer unique opportunities for physical play.

Children's natural curiosity guides what they will learn and they should be encouraged to proceed at their own pace. Learning and development should be personally relevant, with abundant first-hand experience. When children are ready for a particular stage of physical development, they normally choose activities that stimulate and positively affect their growth in that area. If they are not ready for an activity, for example, if they cannot balance on a 5 cm wide beam, they will usually avoid this activity or will learn by trial and error that they are not yet ready.

Talking to Danny, I discovered that he understood fully his stage of development in bike riding. He had come to the playground on his bike with stabilizers, along with his older, bike-riding brother. When asked if he would like to take off the stabilizers today, he said he was not ready to try that yet. He added, 'I'll be ready when I'm 6'.

Jean-Jacques Rousseau said of childhood: 'Is it nothing to skip, to play, to run about all day long? Never in their lives will children be so busy as now' (Santrock 1993: 174). Henry Ward Beecher goes on to suggest 'that energy which makes children hard to

Table 2.1 Some movement development activities

travelling: *walking, jogging, running, hopping along, skipping, hopscotch*

jumping: *along, down, from and on to*

climbing: *up, down, through, along tree, net, pole, ladder, rope*

hanging and swinging: *from hands, hands and feet, back of the knees*

balancing: *along low, wide to high, narrow surfaces*

rocking	rolling	sliding	hiding	building	kite-flying
throwing	catching	pulling	pushing	arranging	collecting
distributing	ordering	manipulating	moulding	feeling	digging
planting	water play	sand play	exploring	seeking	hiding
resting	observing	pedalling	biking	roller-blading	frisbee
yo-yo	marbles				

manage is the energy which afterward makes them managers of life' (Santrock 1993: 241).

The teacher

Providing opportunities for play is a long-established practice in nurseries, pre-school and early years settings, where play and work are seen as integrated elements of child development and learning. In primary schools, play is also encouraged through breaks, which take up a significant part of each day. However, physical play is seen both as a means of letting off steam between sessions of sitting still to engage in academic learning and as a means of repeating, refining and practising motor skills, as well as the important need to have exercise. Challenges to providing the best possible opportunities for physical play in primary schools include ensuring safety, where large numbers of children playing together in a relatively small space, providing sufficient playtime in a school day and resourcing the types of play provision that will meet the play needs of all children.

Cameo 2 illustrates how one school has addressed the challenge of providing appropriate play opportunities by means of a school play scheme, sponsored by local companies and for the provision and maintenance of popular resources for the training of pupils as play leaders to 'manage' the scheme. The main role of the teachers and supervisors in this play organization is to support and facilitate the pupils as play leaders and take overall responsibility. Playtime took on a whole new dimension once the children's previous concerns about not having anything to do and worrying about bullying had been addressed. The play areas were reallocated to provide areas for small games including hopscotch, stilts, skipping and line dancing as aerobic type activities. Areas for short tennis, football and other ball games were organized by play leaders; aiming games, such as skittles and ring toss, were located in their own sectors. This child-centred scheme has greatly increased involvement in physical play, healthy exercise and enjoyment of breaktimes. Concern for maintaining safety had also led to restrictions on permitted activities at playtime, where it is felt that unstructured activity by children could be hazardous. Once the play scheme was in place and the spaces in the playground had been reorganized, this worry faded.

The role of the teachers in this school was to consult the children and then to structure play opportunities for the widest possible range of physical play types and to include in the play environment the greatest possible range of appropriate equipment and resources. Thus playtime is valued as an important part of the school day for the children. In this school traditional games are encouraged, alongside newer activities, so you could expect to see skipping ropes and elastics, basketball and football, stilts, marbles and short tennis.

Playtime there is no longer a neglected aspect of the children's education and the quality of relationships in class is no longer marred by events of playtime, such as conflicts between children. There is no longer a decline in traditional games and the research findings that at playtime, girls tend to lose out on space and equipment, do not apply here.

The school playground has become the main setting for outside play, and it is relatively free from adult intervention to control. Since the school playground may also be one of the few places where children have opportunities to play outside the home, there is increased importance in providing a wide variety of games and activities. This school has recognized the understandable increase in concern by parents of letting children play unsupervised in streets and parks, by providing maximum possible play opportunities within the school environment.

Many teachers admit that they know little about what happens in the playground, since when they are on duty they deal with the immediate events brought to their notice and if not on duty, they tend not to observe children at play. At the Thomas Coram Research Unit, in a study of nearly 200 children aged 7–11 in London, various responses (shown in Table 2.2) were given to the questions 'What do you do now at playtime? How could playtime be improved?'

Those who did not like playtime were put off largely by the weather or because they feared the disruptive behaviour or bullying by other children. To improve the quality of playtime, children requested:

- more permanent equipment such as swings
- an adventure playground
- scramble nets
- climbing frames.

Table 2.2   Playtime survey

Long dinner playtime:	67 boys and 49 girls loved it
	28 boys and 31 girls liked it
	8 children disliked it
	15 children hated it
Morning play:	71% liked or loved it and 15% did not
What was liked about playtime:	41% relaxed and enjoyed the change from work and the chance to have fun
Playing games:	33%
Talking to friends:	32%
Fresh air:	25%
Ball games:	60%
Running round:	15%
Football:	16% specifically noted playing football, of whom 75% were boys and 25% girls

Source: Thomas Coram Institute (1991: 28)

Teachers can be centrally instrumental both in understanding children's play needs and in responding appropriately to meet those needs. The purchase of permanent play structure in one primary school has received popular acclaim by the children (Figure 2.4). Further improvements to playtime were requested by the children in the form of portable equipment, such as balls, bats and frisbees. Other children spoke about a change of use of their school playground. For example it was suggested that boys should have a separate area from girls, that younger children should play at a different time from older children, that there should be space for skateboarding and roller-blading and that there should be better markings to include hopscotch and proper games pitches. Requests also included for the provision of walls to serve as rebound surfaces as well as goals and grass areas with slopes.

Ball games including football were by far the most popular activity, along with netball, basketball, cricket, rugby and rounders. Wall games such as donkey, sevens, aiming and squash-type games were also popular. Chasing games came second in popu-

Figure 2.4   Our new play structure

larity; seeking games, including 'getting back to base' games, were third most popular. Catching games, including tig, tag, games in which players cross space and the catcher intercepts and British Bulldog and racing games in which children set up courses were also reported as favourites. The last significant group of games was skipping games, including rope and elastics, French and Chinese skipping.

Other games were not reported on, possibly due to the seasonal nature of games like marbles, which benefit from fine, warm weather and a dry and clean playing surface for kneeling down to project the marbles on smooth pathways. Conkers feature for a relatively short autumn season and are great fun for practising hand–eye coordination (Figure 2.5).

At one school the willow arch has provided a new dimension to play and to developing skill in fine motor functioning and coordination. Costumed for their history project, the children in Figure 2.6 are teaching each other cat's cradle and using the seclusion of the willow arch area to practise.

Figure 2.5 Natasha and Matthieu honing their conker skills

Where space permits and a school is endowed with extensive asphalt play areas, roller-blading and short tennis are very popular playtime activities for older juniors. In another school children take responsibility for their own protective clothing and knee pads for roller-blading and follow an agreed code of practice for safety. Short tennis is played in another area both for general practice and as a mini-league, with pupil-organized matches at lunchtimes, using six small courts marked on the extensive asphalt area.

If children enjoy playtime it is often not on account of teacher planning. For the most part playtime and playgrounds seem still to be taken for granted by teachers and, apart from minimal supervision, children are left to make what they will of them. This might be one reason why playtime is so popular with children, that is just because it is an alternative to the largely teacher-controlled activities within the school. This would be consistent with the view of Opie and Opie (1969: 128), who made much of the impenetrability to adults into the outside play of children, within which games are passed on from older to younger, the social order is transmitted along with cultural information. Children are the experts on what happens and are often the only

Figure 2.6   Rachel and Jonathan playing cat's cradle by the willow
arch, in costume

witnesses. However, there are a number of ways in which teacher
involvement in playtime and the play area might have a significant effect on the quality of play for many or all children. One
of these is through direct teacher involvement in enhancing
children's play. Teachers can and do enable children to make
better use of playtime and play areas. They may be able to extend
and increase the variety of children's games, or to rearrange the
play area to permit the range of activities that children would
like to play. Then, with the assistance of the community or other
sponsorship, improvements can be made, as at one school which
participated in the 'Health Promoting School' Project and used
some of the grant allocated to invest in improving lunchtime
play opportunities. A second way in which teacher involvement
can improve the quality of play is through sustaining cultural
play. Teachers might introduce children to the playground games
of their youth, recalling some of the 'dips' and rhythm, singing,
stepping or skipping games that they played, or even to reintro-
duce marbles, jacks, boules or pin bowling. Recall games and
games that use playground markings such as 'jump the river'
can create new activities alongside the old. The only proviso is

Figure 2.7 Jordan (aged 8) concentrating on ring toss

that playing must be fun now, and must catch the interest and involvement of the children (Figure 2.7). Teacher involvement is successful only when it is not seen as an intervention into the business of playing.

A third way in which teacher involvement in play could enhance children's physical development is through observation and assessment of what children can do, the quality of the doing and the potential for further enhancing both the movement vocabulary and the skill level of each child. For example, the child who plays football at every playtime, without exception, may become a very able, knowledgeable and skilful footballer, but could also benefit from practising a wider range of movement vocabulary at other times. The child who never engages in physical play at playtime would benefit from greater activity, if only to raise the heart rate and take some exercise, in the interests of health. Children with delayed gross motor development might be encouraged to participate in physical activity during playtimes, through the provision of activities in which they could succeed and feel confident. Information gained from playtime observation by teachers and learning support assistants could also be used as a planning tool for physical education teaching as well as in the planning of classroom activities. The 'knock on' effect of enhanced gross motor competence for all children and particularly those who find fine motor skills difficult cannot be overemphasized. Teachers and carers who observe children's play can acquire a feast of information about the physical child and can then use that information both to enhance children's play experience and to make use of play opportunities to raise each child's level of movement achievement.

Summary

Play is central to children's movement development. Engaging in physical play stimulates both growth and motor development and provides endless opportunities for participatory learning. Ensuring the provision of enjoyable and absorbing indoor and outdoor play, providing opportunities for the development of mature movement patterns in gross and fine motor activities and allocating appropriate time for play are the challenges facing teachers and carers in the twenty-first century.

Questions to ask

1 In what ways does your setting provide play opportunities that enhance children's physical and motor development? How could the environment, equipment and resources be enhanced?
2 What more can you do to take account of gender, ethnic diversity and differing special educational needs in the provision of equal opportunities for gross motor play?
3 In what ways could you develop your role in enhancing children's movement development through play?

3

Language, creativity and physical literacy

Cameo 1

A group of children are talking about their apparatus work in gymnastics. Ricky (aged 10) is learning to climb the rope and says: 'John is teaching me to climb the ropes and he says to keep your hands about 10 centimetres apart and to have a good grip . . . and you need upper body strength. I think you should keep doing it. Practice makes perfect.'

Cameo 2

Sarah and Charlotte (aged 11 years) are coming to the end of the final year in their primary school and are creating a gymnastics floor sequence together, to conclude their unit of work on levels. Sarah describes their work as follows: 'I did a crab and she did a balance over me. She went into a bridge and I slid under her. She rolled over and I did a cartwheel right over her. Sometimes when Charlotte jumped up and things like that, she didn't have straight legs and pointed toes and I said, "Keep your legs straight and point your toes more." She said, "Keep your hands flat", 'cos I keep making a bridge with my hands.'

Cameo 3

In their dance lesson children aged 6 and 7 years are creating their own 'balloon dances' as part of a piece of cross-curricular learning based on the theme of flight. They had worked with a balloon each, to observe its flight and had discussed with their teacher some key words to describe their observations. They had also explored together some movement vocabulary as a starting point for their dances.

Introduction

In the first section of this chapter we consider relationships between movement and language with reference to the child, then the teacher and finally the context. The latter section of the chapter explores some aspects of creativity and relationships between movement and creativity and the implications of movement, language and creativity in the attainment of physical literacy.

Movement and language

Communication of language through movement and communication of movement through language are two of the key elements of this chapter.

Movement gives children access to discovering about the immediate world around them, indeed movement underpins all their learning. For example, babies turn their head to look about, infants reach out with their arms and hands to grasp toys and toddlers crawl around on hands and knees to discover the delights to be found a little further away. It is through movement that the infant explores the environment and through movement that infants and carers develop signals which lead to communication sounds and later to speech. The language–movement triangle (Figure 3.1) illustrates the interrelatedness of language, early movement and physical education. Early movement is a springboard for learning language and is also the basis for children's

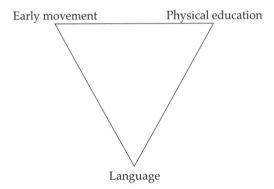

Figure 3.1 The language–movement triangle

physical education. Language is a significant factor in becoming physically educated and PE is an important medium for enhancing language. Both early movement and PE provide a medium for developing movement and language. Language is also integral to learning in PE and both early movement and language are significant in achieving physical literacy.

The child

In young children, movement provides an early medium of communication, well in advance of the development of speech. Infants make their needs known through gesture and movement and they use movement to make demands of others. Parents and carers can pick up signals from the child's movement, which provide communication clues. For example the firm shutting of the mouth as a spoonful of food is presented, or the sharp turning of the head away from the spoon, are clear signals of refusal. The child's arms reaching out towards the carer are usually interpreted as 'Pick me up, please'. In ways such as these children establish an effective communication system through movement, to ensure that their needs are made known. This non-verbal communication system, devised by the child and made up of gestures, is likely to be met, not only with a physical response from the carer, but also with a verbal response. Carers tend to give voice to the movements that the young child uses. They will also have had considerable experience of moving in response to the words that relate to their movement. It may seem that young children can be subjected to a constant verbal accompaniment by their carers. 'Open your mouth' might be the request in response to the firmly closed mouth, refusing food, or 'Do you want to be picked up?' at the sight of the outstretched arms. In fact there are two sorts of monologue that the child might hear. The first is the verbal expression of what the child is doing or is being requested to do, as in 'Clap hands!' when the child is seen to bring the hands together in the mid-line. 'Hold your cup', 'Take off your coat', 'Climb up into bed'. The second is the verbal interpretation of what the carer is doing or is about to do for the child, such as 'Lift you up' or 'Carry you upstairs'. Much of the speech that children hear around them is inevitably centred on what is happening to them, what has happened to them or what is about to happen to them. Movement milestones, or the mastery of a new skill, are also likely to be marked by the carer in language, with much positive feedback on the child's achievements. Thus, 'Clever boy, standing up!' marks that all-important progression towards walking. Carers also use modelling of movement, accompanied by verbal explanations of that model. For example, holding the arms of a child and gently patting the hands together might be accompanied with the words, 'Let's clap hands'.

Another important use made of verbal communication by carers is the naming of the parts of the body that are participating in an activity. This not only establishes for the child the name of the body part engaged in the activity, but also starts to establish an important vocabulary for body awareness, for example 'Sit on your bottom!', 'Open your mouth!', 'Wave your hand!', 'Lift up your foot!'

Once children can bring together relevant verbs, or action words, with the related body part or parts they can begin to create a coherent language of movement. Asher (1983: 3) stated that children decode language through the intimate integration and subsequent relationship of language and bodily movement. This decoding is probably well established before children begin to make their own verbal contributions related to an activity. Bruner (1983: 21) suggests that action, play and movement, which constitute the 'culture of childhood', are crucial to language development. Most children will be talking about what they are doing by the age of 3 years in such a way that their movement and language seem to be interrelated: 'Language is orchestrated to the choreography of the human body' (Asher 1983: 4). A friend of mine, Emma, when she was 5, told me all about the things she could do. She enjoys all physical activity and can run fast, ride a bike, swim, hop and climb. In PE she has learnt sideways rolls and balances in gymnastics, rolling, throwing and catching a ball in games and skipping, twirling and leaping in dance. She wrote down her favourite activities as follow: 'I like climing, hoping and biking'. She too used language 'as orchestration to the choreography of the human body' as she talked about the fine motor activities that she could do, including painting, drawing, cutting out and sticking. Listening to her chatter as she explained everything she was doing, reminded me again of Bruner (1983: 23), who states that 'all utterances have relevance, as the game becomes the topic and the situation provides a contextual conversation'. He continues: 'Movement based interactions provide an environment in which the learner is immersed in understandable messages, where language can be placed in context naturally and meaningfully.'

Vocabulary that is particularly relevant in the context of movement learning includes verbs, prepositions and language related to spatial and body-related aspects of movement development:

behind	above	below	over	under
to the side	in front	around	along	
through	forwards	backwards	sideways	

The teacher

During my childhood physical education was considered to be a 'doing' and not a 'speaking' subject. It was not expected that any pupil would talk during a PE lesson: we were expected to work in silence. Talking was seen as an off-task activity, supposedly detracting from full concentration on the activity in hand and leading to lack of self-control and even to risk of danger. We were told that you cannot do two things at once. Teacher talk during lessons was mainly confined to the giving of instructions and to correction. Then, as now, however, opportunities abound for developing language and for gaining experience in a variety of language-related activities through PE. The teacher uses language to teach movement and also teaches language through children's activities. As movers we need to be able to do at least two things at once, when we move to learn and learn to move. We need to be able to concentrate on the actual movement being performed, to anticipate the next movement, to look around for a safe environment for that movement, to be aware of others sharing the same general space, to memorize the performance in hand and then to reflect on that performance. The contribution of language to refining knowledge and understanding of a piece of work, by giving a verbal description of that work, is a progression in the development towards physical literacy.

In Cameo 2, Sarah and Charlotte are making a 'pairs' sequence in gymnastics (see Maude 1994). Their teacher has encouraged discussion of performance, both through reporting on self-evaluation and reporting on and analysing the work of others. In this excerpt, recorded after the class had been filmed in action, Sarah is well able to describe to the interviewer the content of their sequence. She notes accurately the gymnastics actions that they each performed: 'I did a crab and she did a balance over me. She went into a bridge and I slid under her. She rolled over and I did a cartwheel right over her.' From this description we get a clear picture of what happened during the sequence. We can picture the actions performed, although we cannot tell from the description how those actions were linked. How did Sarah get from the crab into the slide, or from the slide into the cartwheel? We would need to investigate further to complete our internal video of the sequence. However, Sarah offers other information about their work together in her report on the feedback that they gave each other to improve performance. In this way she shows not only the development of a keen eye to observe and be aware of her partner, but also a level of understanding and maturity of language and gymnastics knowledge, from which she draws, to evaluate and articulate that feedback. She records the feedback as follows: 'Sometimes when Charlotte jumped up . . . she didn't have straight legs and pointed toes'. Here is clear evidence for her teacher that Sarah has been able to observe her partner, has noted what she saw and can articulate this, using appropriate and effective vocabulary. Sarah goes further, however, by translating that observation into a specific teaching point for enhancing her partner's performance. She also notes the feedback that her partner gave to her and is able to articulate that knowledge meaningfully to the interviewer, who had not himself been an active participant in the lesson. She reports: 'I said, "Keep your legs straight and point your toes more." She said, "Keep your hands flat", 'cos I keep making a bridge with my hands.' Thus she provides evidence here for engaging in quite complex aspects of the integration of language with movement in the pursuit of physical literacy. I consider that she is developing well her skill in the use of language for descriptive and analytical purposes and would go further, to suggest that she displays another quality here, that of managing to criticize while still supporting the work of her partner. Both children seemed to be physically, intellectually, socially and emotionally comfortable with interacting in this way. There seemed to be an empathy between them in the way in which they worked. This context for learning, by which empathy can heighten awareness and quality of movement, will be discussed further in Chapter 6.

This example nicely demonstrates a series of progressions employed by the teacher, to help her pupils in the use of language to record observation of movement and to translate that observation into verbal communication. These progressions include verbal analysis, feedback on performance, feedforward to future performance and commitment to providing a target for the potential improvement of the next attempt. The teacher uses this important strategy of integration of movement and language to enable the learners to communicate both visually through the movement itself and orally through the language used to service that movement. In this way, physical education offers excellent opportunities for the development of language. Articulate language can also greatly contribute to the enhancement of movement.

Cameo 1 provides another example of the contributions that language can make to movement learning. The teacher of this class of children aged 9 and 10 years was aware that however good she was as a teacher, she could not be 'all-seeing' and 'all-knowing' about every child in the class at all times. She knew the value of peer tutoring both for the child giving feedback and for the learner receiving that feedback. She knew that peer tutoring offers the possibility of more frequent individual tuition by way of formative feedback than can be given by one teacher alone with 32 children. She had taught the children, in the early stages, to follow her lead with regard to which points for development to look for in giving feedback. In this way the children were grounded in what constitutes effective feedback. She had focused on:

- the giving of accurate technical information
- the amount of feedback to give at any one time, if it is to be useful
- the manner of giving feedback if it is to be acceptable to, and user-friendly for, the performer.

In this example, we have access to a dialogue between Ricky and his partner, John. Ricky says: 'John is teaching me to climb the ropes and he says to keep your hands about 10 centimetres apart and to have a good grip . . . and you need upper body strength.' This was useful feedback, since Ricky had been trying to grip the rope with his hands too far apart; this had inhibited his coordination and led to fatigue. The advice about upper body strength is therefore quite pertinent, too! Ricky goes on from the advice from his partner to note also another key factor in the mastery of new or challenging skills: 'I think you should keep doing it. Practice makes perfect.'

The concept of speech being interpreted through movement is one of the unique qualities of teaching and learning in physical education. Unlike any other subject in the school curriculum, except perhaps drama, movement is the output from a task set by the teacher using words. This can be quite a challenge for teachers, whose responsibility it is to elicit movement of the required style, quantity and quality intended from the verbal instruction. It is also a challenge for the learner, to make sense of those words and to translate them into acceptable movement which both fulfils the teacher's task and demonstrates an ever-improving level of performance. In the average class of children of mixed ability, there may be some children for whom the instructions are difficult to understand and others who understand the instructions but who find it difficult to use them to work to the best of their ability. Yet other children may prefer to take time to consider the task set before starting to move. However, the teacher might interpret such inactivity as non-participation, since most children will already be working with the task through movement.

A group of trainee teachers discovered that finding ways of setting tasks in a clear, unambiguous way, while at the same time providing challenge for all the children, was a skill that needed much practice. They knew that the children should be spending the majority of the lesson engaged in physical activity, rather than listening to the teacher or becoming confused by not being able to understand the task set. Since movement is the main medium of learning in PE, the trainees wanted to find language that was succinct and clear, so that the children could subsume the instruction into their ongoing movement development. As Blake (1996: 5) says: 'A process of communication needs to be established which guarantees that information is given clearly, concisely and accurately.' Part of the establishing of that process of communication is to teach children to listen to, and to pay attention to, the words that they hear and to make meaning for themselves from those words. Extending children's listening skills and their understanding of language through listening, in order to make sense of the teacher's verbal communication is an important role of the teacher.

Another role is to extend children's language through talking, since speech is one way of ascertaining the level of knowledge achieved through an episode of teaching, as seen in the cameos above. Children's talk during PE lessons should include:

- answering questions
- asking questions
- describing movement observed
- explaining their own movement
- analysing the movement of others
- giving feedback on their analysis of that movement
- suggesting ways to improve that movement
- using the technical language of that activity
- using vocabulary for creative movement
- confirming knowledge of techniques and progressions
- proposing new movement, strategies, tactics or ways of working
- demonstrating their understanding of health and safety in movement.

Dance offers a special opportunity to use and to interpret language, by drawing on and developing the more creative aspects of movement. In dance, the language used should include descriptive words and phrases to which the children can relate. Words such as those below have been found to provide the stimulus for more expressive movement:

whirl	shrink	slither	glide	leap	bound
spin	crawl	gather	scatter	dash	soar
drag	pause	crouch	burst	whip	plunge
zigzag	tremble	skim	throw	rock	hop
skip	wander	toss	twirl	press	push
tiptoe	creep	collapse	expand	clap	rise
fall	shrivel	close	open	flutter	encircle
hover	arch	sway	wander	settle	crumble
twist	turn	shatter	run		

Source: adapted from Homerton College PE Department (1998: 79)

For example, children could choreograph a short dance based on the following six words, aiming to express those words in movement vocabulary: 'whirl, twirl, swirl; shrink, settle and melt'.

The dance might be expected to be in two parts, starting with a lively travelling and wide-gestured series of travelling, turning and jumping actions to convey the first three words, and followed by a slowing to stillness as the dancer lowers to the ground and comes to a pause. Children might chant the words to provide an accompaniment to their sequence or to add atmosphere to their dance.

The use of poetry for dance not only provides a stimulus, but also challenges the dancers to interpret the vocabulary of the poet within their dance. For example, Robert Southey's poem *The Cataract of Lodore* (see Dane 1978) contains key movement words such as 'eddying and whisking', 'darting and parting'. Some children find a stimulus such as this helps them to interpret a text and thus enhance and extend their understanding of the expressive qualities of their movement and of dance as a discrete discipline. They may set the dance to music or to a rhythm composed by themselves or might use a reading of the poem to accompany the dance.

In Cameo 3, the children used balloons as the starting point for their dance. Having tried out what they could make the balloon do and observed the flight of their balloon, they suggested words to describe what they had done and what they had seen in the movement of the balloon (Figure 3.2). Having pushed the balloon into the air and along the ground, they squeezed the balloon in their arms and let go before it burst. They also blew up their balloon and let it go undone, so that it flew around the room causing much excitement. Several children were brave enough to burst their balloon and watch it disappear to the ground! They suggested the following vocabulary as the starting point for their dances:

floating, bouncing, batting, rolling, whizzing, jetting, flying, jumping jacks, zooming, jumping, shrivelling, falling, smoothly, pressing, hitting, blowing, getting bigger, getting smaller, roundy, bitty, quickly, above, down, behind, away.

The teacher and children together selected the following words to try out in movement, to give the children a basic movement vocabulary, as a starting point for their dance. They chose 'floating, smoothly, above, down, zooming and shrivelling'. The children

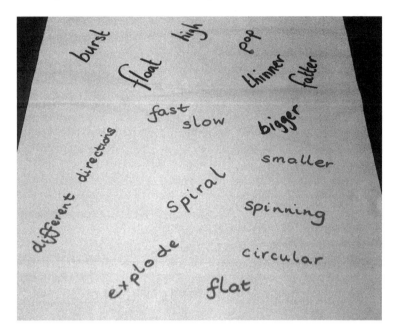

Figure 3.2 Our balloon words

then chose other words to include in their own movement phrase and the idea of a dance with a three-part structure was then introduced. The dance started with all the children working together on the first four words; this was followed by the phrase of movement that each child had prepared and then the dance ended with all the children dancing together again using the 'zooming and shrivelling' phrase previously practised. The teacher went on to improve the quality of the dance, including the timing, the coordination of the two whole class elements and the organization and timing of the individual dances (Figure 3.3).

The context

Carers often respond to the movement of infants by using words to describe to them that movement. Achievement of movement milestones are most likely to be reported in language and much positive feedback to infants and young children arises as a result of vocabulary and language applicable to moving. In nursery,

Figure 3.3   Our balloon dance

pre-school and primary school settings, practitioners and teachers
use language as a means of providing for the activities of the day,
including administration, instruction, explanation, task setting and
feedback. Much of what they say requires a movement response
from the children, if only to put up their hand, to return to their
seats, to line up at the door, to take off their coats, or to engage in
the many fine motor tasks that make up the school day.

The National Curriculum for England and Wales (DfEE 1999:
38) indicates the requirement to teach writing, speaking, listening and reading across the curriculum as appropriate. The final
statement is:

> Pupils should be taught the technical and specialist vocabu-
> lary of subjects and how to spell these words. They should be
> taught to use the patterns of language vital to understand-
> ing and expression in different subjects.

In physical education, there are at least nine categories of
vocabulary that can usefully contribute both to children's language development and to their physical education. These are:

- body awareness vocabulary
body limbs, e.g. leg, arm
body joints, e.g. shoulders, elbow, wrist, fingers, hip, knee, ankle, foot
body organs, e.g. heart and lungs, so important in exercise
relationship words, e.g. hands shoulder-width apart, feet together, flat hands
- environment vocabulary
hall, gym, field, hard-play area, pitch, court, track, swimming pool, sports hall, playground
- resource, apparatus, equipment vocabulary
game type includes beanbag, bat, ball, shuttle, stick, tee
dance type includes cymbal, tambour, poem, CD, tape recorder, video, mirror, digital camera
gymnastics type includes mat, rope, bench, ramp, bar box, fixed apparatus
athletics type includes measuring tape, take-off point, stop-watch
outdoor and adventurous activity type includes control, compass
swimming includes float, rail
- spatial vocabulary
over, under, up, down, forwards, backwards, sideways, high, medium, low, near to, far from
- temporal vocabulary
slowly, accelerate, quickly, decelerate, pause, stop
- motor skill vocabulary
jump, catch, throw, kick, run, float, go, stop, vault, climb, travel
- movement quality vocabulary
fluently, resiliently, lightly, strongly, with body tension, with extension
- physical education vocabulary
acquire, develop, select, apply, evaluate, improve, composition, fitness, health, safety
- physical education activity-specific vocabulary
games, teams, travel, send, receive, invasion, net-wall, strike-field, tactics, attack, defence
dance, choreography, dancer, stimulus, composition
gymnastics, rotation, flight, inversion, floor, apparatus, sequence

The first two of the National Curriculum language requirements, to teach speaking and listening, are readily developed in physical

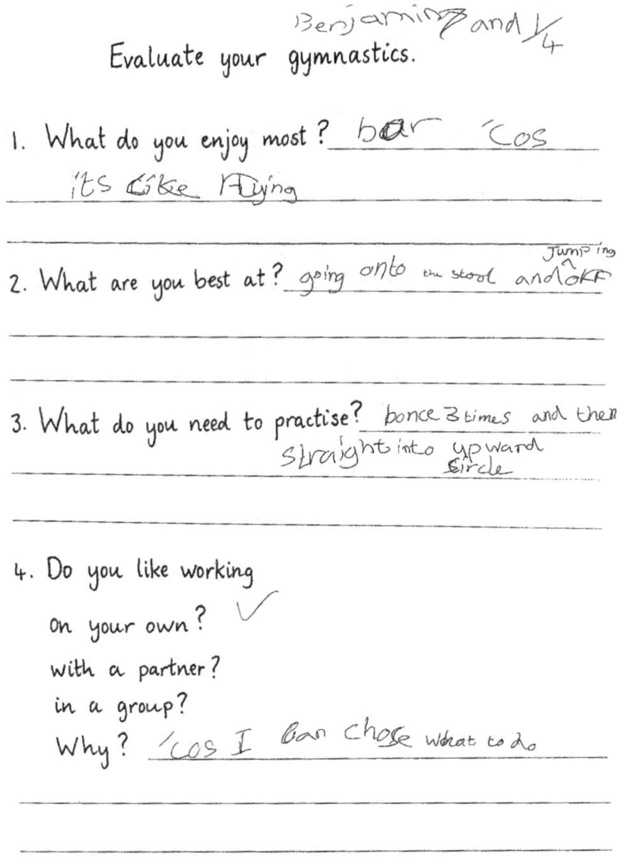

Evaluate your gymnastics.   *Benjamin and 1/4*

1. What do you enjoy most ? bar cos
   its like flying

2. What are you best at ? going onto the stool and off *Jumping*

3. What do you need to practise? bonce 3 times and then
   straight into upward circle

4. Do you like working
   on your own ? ✓
   with a partner ?
   in a group?
   Why ? cos I Can chose what to do

Figure 3.4   Ben's (aged 7) gymnastics evaluation

education, as has been demonstrated. Reading and writing can also be incorporated, as shown in the examples of children's work in Chapter 4. A further example is shown in Figure 3.4, in which Ben (aged 7) writes his evaluation of his learning in gymnastics.

Movement and creativity

The concept of creativity is often considered to be complex and attainable in movement only by articulate, skilful and experienced movers. As Best (1985: 89) said: 'A necessary condition for being creative is to have mastered at least to some extent the discipline, techniques and criteria of a subject or activity.'

However, Arnold (1970: 84) said: 'Play is basically a creative function of child behaviour.' He also described play as the natural medium for self-expression. He suggested that play helps with the development of self, it helps acquaint the child with reality and helps the process of self-realization and integration (Arnold 1970: 80). The concept of creativity as represented here, stemming from, and integrated into, the child's world of play, is exactly the concept of creativity that we should be encouraging in young children. I would venture to suggest that the young child, as an expert in playfulness, could be seen to possess the conditions proposed by Best (1985) in relation to play. Stemming from imaginative play, children can express aspects of creativity through their playful movement. Young children show in their spontaneous, expressive, uninhibited naivety a special freedom of movement which is so often lost in middle childhood. Young children indulge in movement, they are constantly creating new movement from their rich experience.

'Let creativity shape the future!' was the appeal of Jude Kelly (1998). In looking at the world of the future, rather than at the world of today or yesterday, she acknowledges that what will be needed in the society of the future are 'civic-minded citizens, multi-disciplined, with flexible, transferable skills, entrepreneurial and capable of adapting to the hectic speed of change'. She goes on to suggest that it is those teachers who argue for creativity to be an entitlement for all children do so because of the overwhelming evidence that 'Allowing expressiveness and imaginative curiosity to flourish, creates a level of confidence, self-esteem and purposefulness that can change a child's abilities for ever.'

The arts should be studied in their own right and also because the qualities that the arts disciplines offer can bring great benefits when applied to other subjects. Kelly claims that creative approaches to dreaming unlock motivation and enthusiasm, develop lateral thinking and encourage independence of thought, allowing children to deal with a changing world. By contrast, literacy, numeracy and computer skills will not provide them with the range of knowledge and ingenuity needed to take them into a dynamic future.

In his lecture to the Royal Society, Elliot Eisner (1998) urged that schools should not become boot camps for learning how to make a living, but places for learning how to make a life. How can teachers address this need, given the statutory demands made on the curriculum? How can space be made for the arts and for the nurturing of creative experience? Davis (1971: 221) proposes that the best way to promote creativity in children is by means of creative teaching. He suggests that creative teachers provide for self-initiated learning, encourage creative thinking, engage children in experimentation and hypothesis, promote intellectual flexibility and help children to seek new connections and to take intellectual risks. The provision of a non-threatening environment, in which open-ended questions foster curiosity and open up alternatives, in which the learners cope with frustration and failure and where they are urged to consider problems as wholes, rather than as piecemeal elements, also make way for creativity to flourish.

The implications for movement education and particularly for dance are profound. Eisner (1972: 43) claims: 'The Arts teach children how to exercise judgement and how to cope with the unexpected. They teach children that sensitive attention to relationships is critical, that problems can have more than one solution and questions more than one answer.' Eisner further suggests that dance should be both a process and a product and that children should learn to 'delve into their poetic capacities to invent a language that will do the job'. The Early Learning Goals (QCA 1999a: 39) for children in the foundation stage of their education (aged 3–7 years), contain a whole section on creative development. The activities represented in this section include dance, music, imaginative play, role play and art. It is claimed that 'Creativity is fundamental to successful learning'. 'Being creative enables children to make connections between one area of learning and another and so extend learning.' Practitioners should provide a rich environment in which creativity and expressiveness are valued and where the use of the senses is encouraged. Time should be given for developing ideas and activities planned which are both enjoyable and imaginative.

By the time children move into Key Stage 1 at 5 years of age, creativity is notable by its absence in the National Curriculum. There is a section on problem-solving, but it does not detail the creative development necessary. It seems as if the creative development necessary for problem-solving had already been mastered and is therefore taken for granted. Within the Key Skills section on Thinking Skills, there are two lines suggesting that creative thinking skills enable pupils to generate and extend ideas, to hypothesize, to apply imagination and to look for alternative innovative outcomes (DfEE 1999: 22). This small statement opens the door for a physical education curriculum that uses all the means available to teach creatively, so that children learn to use movement creatively and become confident in the creative and expressive aspects of physical education. In Chapter 6 further reference will be made to the development of creativity by the active teacher and the active learner.

Summary

Movement development can often be seen to focus on motor skills, those essential components of the competent, efficient, well-coordinated mover. However, the whole range of movement vocabulary upon which to draw to explore and develop expressive and creative movement is an important aspect of children's curriculum as they work towards physical literacy. Using movement to learn language and increasing vocabulary to learn movement are also important tools in the acquisition of physical literacy.

Questions to ask

1 In your setting what provision is there for children to explore and develop creative movement?
2 Draw up a schedule to record the range and extent of children's movement language and use of technical movement vocabulary to explain their actions.
3 In what ways could you enhance the environment, resources, planning in your setting, to extend the children's creative movement experience and their vocabulary to explain their movement learning?

4

Movement observation and assessment

Robbie (aged 5) had been avidly studying a video of the batting styles of cricketers in the World Cup, before he and his

Figure 4.1   Robbie (aged 5) takes strike

brother Adam kitted up for a training session. Robbie was in to bat and took time, as all professionals do, to prepare his wicket, to adjust his stance and grip of the bat, to rehearse his back swing, strike and follow-through and to look around at the field, before settling to watch the arrival of the ball (Figure 4.1).

Cameo 2

Mrs B is encouraging the children in her infant classroom to improve their fine motor skills. *She* has set up a battery of activities to give the children practice in hand–eye coordination and is observing their competence as she and her class helpers give individual assistance to the learners. She uses her observations as diagnostic assessment and to inform her of the children's abilities and potential for success in activities which call for fine motor skill competence.

Cameo 3

Rafael (aged 10) whose first language is Spanish, wrote an assessment of his gymnastics lesson in which the children were asked to show by the size of their smile, the amount of achievement that they felt they had made in the various learning activities of their gymnastics lesson (Figure 4.2).

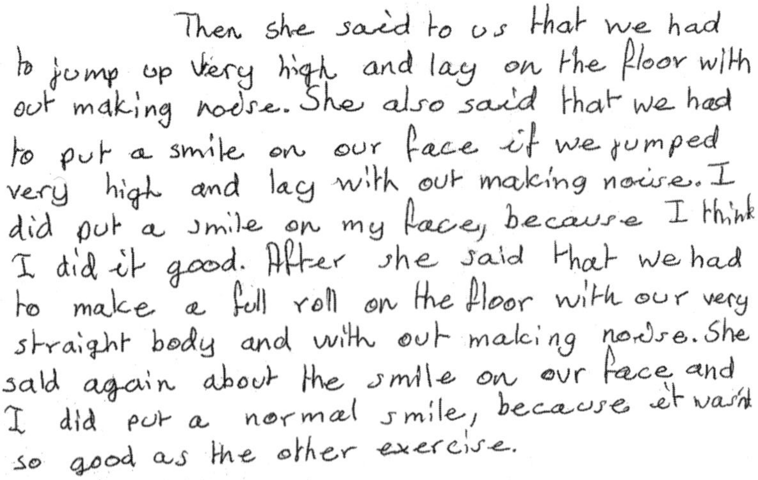

Then she said to us that we had to jump up very high and lay on the floor with out making noise. She also said that we had to put a smile on our face if we jumped very high and lay with out making noise. I did put a smile on my face, because I think I did it good. After she said that we had to make a full roll on the floor with our very straight body and with out making noise. She said again about the smile on our face and I did put a normal smile, because it wasn't so good as the other exercise.

Figure 4.2 Extract from Rafael's (aged 10) written assessment

Introduction

Movement observation is an invaluable tool in constant use by children and their teachers. Movement observation also becomes an ability which, if developed and used effectively in conjunction with assessment and feedback, can vastly enhance children's achievements.

This chapter is about children and their teachers developing and refining skills of observation and honing their ability to use assessment to advantage. Through effective use of observation and assessment children can be helped to acquire an ever-increasing movement vocabulary, can learn to move confidently and imaginatively with increasing control and coordination and can strive to become ever more physically literate and skilful. This chapter is also about the contribution that effective observation and accurate and appropriate assessment can make in ensuring that children continue to gain movement mastery and to reach their potential with confidence. Skilful teacher and peer observation, along with appropriate teacher assessment, peer assessment and ipsative (self-assessment), are powerful tools in extending and enhancing the quality and range of children's movement competence and in developing the quality and richness of the child's movement vocabulary.

Questions that teachers have asked to help children attain their potential in movement competence and knowledge include:

- When, what and how should we observe?
- What should we expect to see, from our observation, that is significant about children's developing movement competence?
- What, how and when should we assess and for what purpose?
- How should we observe children in order to assess and set targets for further movement development, so that we can help them to be more effective learners?
- How can we teach children about what, when and where to observe, in order that they gain and then use effectively the observation information acquired?
- How can children learn to self-assess productively?

Another intention within this chapter, then, is to take account of these questions and to propose some frameworks for observation and assessment both for the child, the teacher and the context of learning.

The child

Observation

Observation, according to the *Concise Oxford Dictionary* (1988), is an aptitude for, and competence in, taking notice, while to be observant is to be attentive, acute or diligent in taking notice. Taking notice and then developing these qualities of attentiveness, acuteness and diligence are extremely valuable in the process of using observation techniques to learn and to teach skilful movement.

David (1999: 134) suggests that observation is of vital importance to children's learning because it enables them to focus, question and develop broader understanding of scientific processes. So also is observation vital in the acquisition and understanding of movement skills and principles and the application of these to the multitude of movement demands that children encounter on a daily basis. The infant takes notice through observation from quite a young age and is increasingly more successful in using that observation to achieve manipulative skills such as grasping an object, as the mechanism in the eyes and the muscles of the limbs mature. However, to increase accuracy, for example, in piling objects up on one another, the skill of observation needs to be enhanced sufficiently that the child takes notice of details that previously were missed, including the lowering of one object on to the greatest possible amount of the surface area of the object below, as well as noting the correct moment for release of each object (Figure 4.3).

Discovering that trial and error is just one way of increasing experience and that observing and copying is another, provides children with at least two techniques for learning. A further enhancement of observation is learning to look more closely and take notice of just a part of the whole event, to analyse and apply just the key element or elements that will increase success. For example, watching the thrower and the thrower's total action of sending a ball, rather than focusing on the object thrown, results in a 'hit and miss' of success in catching a ball, whereas watching the missile, and the flight of the missile all the way to the hands, results in much greater likelihood of success. Similarly, in throwing overarm towards a target, the learner can improve in accuracy by watching examples of accurate throwing and by selecting to

Figure 4.3   Le Le (aged 3) carefully adds another block

observe closely both the point of release of the missile along the trajectory of the thrower's hand as well as the follow-through of the throwing arm and hand.

Interestingly, in observing a performance, children usually see the outcome of that performance first and from that they are able to judge whether the performance was successful or not. They are well able to report on the result that the performance was or was not successful, but usually have much greater difficulty in observing to give an account of why a performance failed. For example, if a rolled ball passed to the side of the target, the child can report: 'the ball missed the target' or 'the ball went to the side of the target' or 'the ball went in the wrong direction', but may not be able to report that this was caused by the stance or that the preparation and action themselves were not accurate.

A first principle of observation is that 'what you see at the end of an action is just a part of the story'. Helping children to understand that the evidence gained from the end product needs to be tracked back through the entire performance to find the source of any error. The outcome itself is just partial evidence. Learning to analyse each of the three linked phases making up movement actions, namely the preparation, the action and the recovery, is quite a challenging task for the inexperienced!

Look at Theo (aged 9) preparing to perform a forward roll along a bench (Figure 4.4). He has learnt from observing success-ful performers that success depends not only on the preparatory stance for the roll, but also the lifting of the hips, bending of the elbows, lowering of the shoulders rather than the head on to the bench and rolling straight down the spine before placing the feet carefully in line and bringing the hips and shoulders over the feet to stand up. He knows that the initial preparation provides the basis for success and that he must align his feet, knees, hips, eyes, shoulders, elbows and hands, directly above and in line with the bench, so that the action flows out of a streamlined and accurate starting position. He has taken notice of the parts of the roll that precede the actual element of rocking down the spine and placing the feet to stand. He has also practised separately the final part, 'rocking down the spine and placing the feet to stand up' (Figure 4.5), knowing that once the ending is perfect, it is much easier to add the start of the roll and to succeed (Figure 4.6).

A second principle of observation is that children are often more able to observe differences than similarities in performance. For example, if the demonstrator performs a perfect forward roll, children working on that technique will more than likely declare it to be a good roll, but may not be able to say why or to compare it with their own performance. If, instead, the demonstrator per-forms a good forward roll but with bent knees in the rolling phase, the learners will recognize and explain the error in the knees as a deviation from the best performance. They can then be shown the roll with extended knees and can then concentrate on that element in their own performance.

A third principle of observation, which can be illustrated using the example above, is that of 'whole-part-whole' learning, whereby the activity to be learnt is shown in its entirety, followed by a demonstration of part of the technique only, in this case the rock-ing section, with bent and then with straight knees. This part is then practised with straight knees (Figure 4.5), before the entire roll is again demonstrated and practised.

Figure 4.4   Theo (aged 9) preparing to roll

Figure 4.5   Theo rocking with straight knees

Figure 4.6   Theo completing the roll

It is interesting to note that not every child will see the same thing when observing movement, since each child may have concentrated on a different aspect of the total performance. For example, in the leap from one foot to the other, some children, particularly those in the early stages of mastering the skill, find the landing on one foot to be difficult and therefore watch that part. Others more experienced may focus on the postural position in the air, or on the use of the arms to aid elevation and flight. This reinforces the importance of focusing the learners' observation on the aspect being targeted, such as the take-off, flight phase or landing and within each phase, the action or position of the body, the upper limbs or the lower limbs. It is also important to give learners the opportunity to articulate what they have observed and to explore in language as well as in movement some strategies for improving performance.

Even very young children learn through observation. Indeed much of children's movement learning comes by trial, success and error, and through watching and attempting to copy the actions of others, whether it be a parent or as below, another child. Thereafter, the greatest aspiration for very young children may be the achievement of mature movement patterns in the basic gross motor activities, since the mastery of these will provide a reliable source of competent movement vocabulary to apply with confidence to the myriad of daily activities and to the world of play, so important in children's development.

Note how in Figure 4.7 the younger child is watching and copying the body shape of the older. Though little awareness seems to be shown at the leg end, which would be in keeping with cephalo-caudal development, great effort is being made to hold a strong body with wide arms.

The physical child comes to the threshold of education armed with a wealth of motor skills and movement abilities that have matured through nurture and practice throughout the early years and which are available, at the child's disposal, to be applied as and when needed in educational settings. Some skills are not as well developed, however, as they may have lain dormant due to lack of opportunity for practice. Alternatively, they may not yet have emerged, because the 'moment of readiness' has not been reached, perhaps due to lack of body preparation or to inadequate mastery of the progressions that could lead to the acquisition of those skills. For example, the 'moment of readiness' for riding

Figure 4.7   We are making star shapes

a bike can result from many progressions, or elements which together enable the 'bike-off-without-fall-off' stage to be achieved. These include maturation of the balance-achieving mechanisms in the ears, strength in the arms and hands to grip the handlebars and control direction, strength in the legs and body to maintain upright posture and turn the pedals and overall body coordination, to combine all these actions together and keep the body and bike upright, while propelling the bike forward! Progressions for bike riding might also include knowledge of pedal turning, the confidence to set off and stop with control and prior experience gained from driving a go-kart (Figure 4.8) or managing a scooter, riding a tricycle (Figure 1.8) or a two-wheeler with stabilizers.

Yet other skills, in which most children have the ability to be proficient by the time they start school, may not have emerged due to lack of exposure. For example, most children are physically capable of swimming by the age of 4 and often earlier, but without having watched others swimming and without also having repeated access to safe, warm water and the encouragement, support, commitment and persistence of carers, they may have to rely on the school curriculum to provide opportunities for

Figure 4.8 Jamie (aged 2) is already a proficient go-karter

learning to swim. Such opportunities may not become available in school until at least the age of 7, due to the many other demands on the school curriculum.

In Cameo 1, Robbie (aged 5) shows how very aware and highly motivated he is when it comes to physical competence. With two older brothers, themselves active sportsmen, he has the added stimulus of two ever-present role models, both of whom are supportive and patient teachers and both of whom he also watches practising and playing in teams. Robbie knows what he can do now, what he can aspire to and will be able to do soon and he is also proud to have earned a place in the village junior football squad, well ahead of the normal age of admission. Although Robbie is an exceptional footballer who says he is best at defence and goalkeeping, he knows he is also good at cricket, rugby, throwing and catching a ball and wrestling. His most recent acquisition is a tennis racket and although he has already made a start, he says that he is not good at tennis yet.

Watching Robbie practising, it is abundantly clear that he is terrifically self-motivated, has excellent body and spatial awareness and coordination, and a well-proportioned body, body strength and muscle tension. Above all he has a very keen eye, learns from what he sees and readily assesses his achievements and aspirations.

Observation is a vital tool for many children as they learn new movement skills and as they learn to move efficiently. In physical education copying or modelling is now a recognized technique within the National Curriculum for 2000 in England. Children are specifically taught to observe and to copy the movement of others from the start of their schooling. Strategies for observation to plan into the physical education curriculum might include the following:

- watch and copy the teacher or other more able performer
- watch and copy a partner
- copy a partner to learn to synchronize movement in gymnastics or dance, to work as a mirror image of one another, as a pair
- look at and copy still photo, digital photo projected, or watch and copy a piece of video or a projected CD-ROM
- work with large screen projection of movement to be learnt
- work with a mirror
- video a piece of movement work and replay it to observe for immediate feedback
- use PowerPoint and other ICT tools.

Assessment

The School Examination and Assessment Council (SEAC 1991: 15) states that pupils can be actively involved in their own assessment: reviewing their work and progress; setting targets for future learning; and deciding in discussion with teachers, which pieces of work provide evidence of particular attainment. This is eminently the case in movement learning and in physical education. The following examples illustrate various methods of pupil self-assessment and peer assessment, collected from a selection of gymnastics lessons with children aged from 5 to 11, in a variety of school settings in Britain and in Spain.

Oral reporting and peer tutoring orally is the most common form of assessment following episodes of observation in physical education. Julie (aged 10) reports on her own progress in jumping and landing when she says: 'I used to just jump and you heard a big bang, now you can't hear anything, it is just so soft' (Maude 1994). Also in the *Gym Kit* video, David (aged 11) is assessing and peer tutoring Emily (also aged 11) in the task set by the teacher of helping a partner to improve. Having observed her sequence he reports: 'On your arabesque balance you went a bit wobbly, like this.' He shows her a wobbly arabesque and then, while describing a more stable arabesque, he also demonstrates what he means. She listens and watches him closely and then goes on to practise her arabesque several times, showing distinct improvement. He then asks her to incorporate the new learning into the sequence.

By way of making a written record of their self-assessment, a group of children were given a chart on which to draw their achievements and areas for development in gymnastics. The chart encouraged them to record examples of very good work, good work and work that needed practice. They had been learning to extend their knees and ankles while working on the apparatus.

Jenny (aged 5) records very accurately her knowledge of her straight knees and ankles, showing her very good work on familiar apparatus and the areas needing practice, understandably, on unstable and high apparatus (Figure 4.9). Lauren's assessment

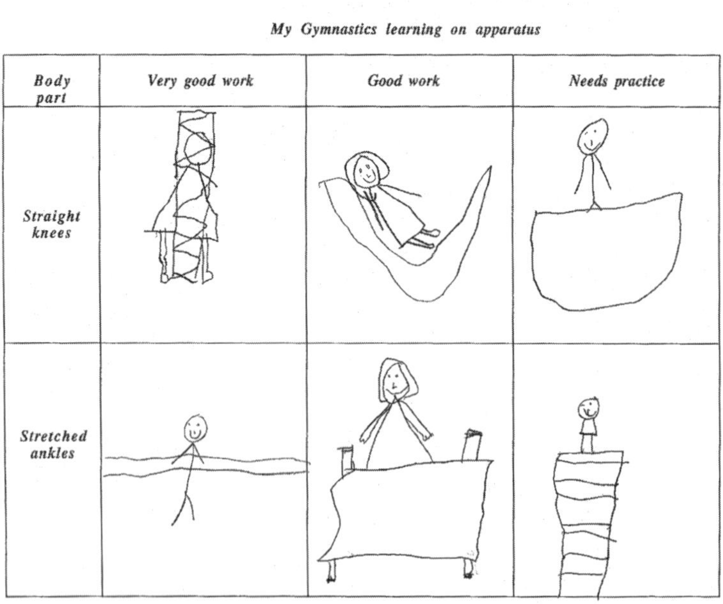

My Gymnastics learning on apparatus

Body part	Very good work	Good work	Needs practice
Straight knees			
Stretched ankles			

Figure 4.9   Jenny's (aged 5) gymnastics assessment

is a much more detailed and sophisticated record (Figure 4.10). Interestingly she was often to be seen working upside-down, although she chose not to record any examples on her chart. She explained that this was because it was very difficult to know what was happening to her knees and ankles when she was upside-down. As with Jenny, Lauren (aged 8) records that she needs more practice on unstable apparatus like 'the jelly'. Lauren also includes, for further practice, activities involving the complexities of flight, such as vaulting over the 'horse' and controlling her body in the air to maintain straight knees during the flight phase of a jump on the 'trampette'. Interestingly, Lauren records as 'good' (in the top box of the chart) her ability to work with straight knees on the pommels of the horse. When comparing this with her performance (shown in Figure 4.11) photographed on the same day, one wonders what she feels she needs to do to achieve a 'very good' in her self-assessment!

Rafael (aged 10), whose self-assessment smile is described in Cameo 3, writes a summary of his learning in his gymnastics lesson. He accompanies his record with two lively illustrations of his gymnastics learning (Figure 4.12).

My Gymnastics learning on apparatus

Body part	Very good work	Good work	Needs practice
Straight knees	rope / box	horse / jelly	horse / bouncer
Stretched ankles	tubo / rocker	silver bar / bouncer	box / jelly

Figure 4.10 Lauren's (aged 8) gymnastics assessment

Figure 4.11   Look at my straight knees!

The final example is by Robert (aged 11), who had been learning both to assess his own progress in linking gymnastics actions into a sequence and also to peer tutor another child. He was then asked to record what he had been taught about linking and sequences in gymnastics, to assess what he had achieved and to suggest what he believed he should learn next (Figure 4.13). His record demonstrates very good gymnastics knowledge and he shows rigour in both the assessment of what he has achieved and what he will go on to learn. The record also suggests that both his observation skills and his self and peer assessment experience is very competent for a child of his age and that he is appropriately challenged in his gymnastics learning.

Teacher observation and assessment

Observation

Of teacher observation, Ofsted (1996c: 5) reported in the *Survey of Good Practice*: 'Acute observation skills, good judgements of when

This week I learned with Miss Maud how to jump up very high, and lay on the floor without making a noise, how to roll with our straight body with out making noise, to run quietly and how to make some good movements with our straight body.

Figure 4.12 Rafael's (aged 10) summary in words and pictures

to intervene in the learning process, clear feedback, with thoughtfully sharp comment, all contributed to effective performance and progress in pupils' understanding.'

Movement is not easy to observe analytically because it leaves no trace, as writing and painting do. Movement is transitory and in most children's general experience is not repeatable, being most usually exploratory and not committed to movement memory. Learning to observe in order to give feedback or to assess quality of performance is a key skill for the trainee teacher. A good starting point is to observe repetitive movement, such as skipping along or skipping with a rope, running or swimming, since the repetitious nature of the movements allow us to 'get our eye in' and to interrogate the quality of the performance as a whole, as well as each aspect of the performance, as it occurs. By contrast, it is most difficult to observe and absorb the quality of the particular

My Gymnastics Assessment on Linking and Sequences

Name _____   Class _____

What I was taught	What I achieved	What I will try to learn next
to link gymnastic actions	linking jumps, rolls, balances and travel	to include unusual twists as links
to make a sequence of 6 linked actions	jump half turn (1), lower to sit to shoulder balance (2), fish flop to front lie, dish roll (3), press up to front support jump to feet, kettle stand (4), 3 travelling bunny jumps, forward roll (5), run and leap (6), lower to end in crouch	to make my sequence more dynamic and exciting by going from high to low twice and by balancing upside down on my hands
to include contrast in speed, direction, body shape and levels in the sequence	I included fast and slow, high and low, forwards and backwards	I need to include more asymmetry in my body shapes
to teach my partner	to watch my partner and say what was good	learn how to help my partner to link more smoothly
to assess my own work to improve it	I learnt to listen to my landings and make them quieter and to keep my sequence going	I need to make each action perfect as well as keeping my sequence flowing

Figure 4.13   Robert's (aged 11) chart to record self-assessment of linking in gymnastics

movement content of a game, since by their very nature, games are not predictable. Similarly it is relatively difficult to commit to observation memory the exploratory stages of a gymnastics sequence or the expressive qualities when observing a dance.

Another helpful starting point for beginner teachers in movement observation is to notice the most agile and the least agile children in the class and, using these extremes, to start to discriminate between those who differ less markedly. In the Ministry of Education (1953) publication *Planning the Programme*, we read on page 25: 'Every teacher who knows which are the most agile and which the exceptionally awkward children in his [*sic*] class has already begun to observe movement.' From this starting point the next progression might be to note particular features of the most able performer which appear to contribute to the quality of that performance, then to share those aspects with the whole class, thereby giving everyone something to look out for in others and to concentrate upon for themselves. *Planning the Programme* further suggests:

> If as a result of observing many different activities the teacher can establish lines of observation, he will be able not only to coach certain kinds of performance, but also to help both the vigorous and the lethargic, the jerky and the even, the heavy as well as the light, the angular as well as the rounded.
> (Ministry of Education 1953: 25)

The three principles for observation which were discussed in the opening section of the chapter, in relation to the child, apply equally well to the teacher. The first of these is that 'what you see is not the whole story'. For example, when we observe children missing the ball every time they attempt to hit it, we may not have noticed that the failure was the result of stance and early preparation, rather than a failure to watch the oncoming flight of the ball. We tend to see the point at which the failure occurs, rather than the source. Second, it is often easier to observe differences than similarities in performance, and third, when a 'whole-part-whole approach' is taken to learning a skill, the observer has greater opportunities for diagnostic analysis. A fourth principle, often adopted by teachers to help children to see more clearly the desired response, is known as 'exaggerated correction'. Here the example to be copied is a larger than life version of the actual performance required. Through attending to the detail of the exaggerated performance, learners are often able to replicate the correct element of the performance.

Learning to teach from observation is an essential and yet often challenging skill for many trainee and practising teachers alike, especially in physical education, since movement is available for observation only fleetingly; with many children moving at the same time, it seems to be almost impossible to isolate and focus on each individual child. So often it seems that, just at the crucial moment when essential information needs to be shared with a learner, either the child cannot remember the performance or the movement of other learners seems to crowd out the previous observation! Knowing when to target observation, in order to give immediate, informed feedback on current performance so that subsequent, appropriately developmental tasks can be provided, is a valuable achievement for the teacher. Observing in mathematics needs time, according to de Bóo (1999: 19), who cites the need for time for exploration and investigation, time for describing and thinking aloud and time for recording what has been seen. These factors pertain just as much to observation of physical activity, both for the teacher and for the learner. Learning what to select to observe is a challenge for both learner and teacher! For the learner participating in a game of catch and throw, watching the flight of an oncoming ball, its speed, direction and level are crucial, but how often do children find themselves watching the face or hand of the sender, rather than the ball, thereby missing crucial information about its arrival and then failing to catch? Knowing what to focus on and when is a great challenge for the young observer.

In the session described below a group of trainee teachers demonstrated many sound observational skills as they took time to work with a child, exploring, investigating, discussing and coaching a skill, then analysing and recording the performance of that child. They were learning not only what, when and how to observe but also how to use that observation for formative, diagnostic and summative assessment and recording. The trainees were following a course on the physical and motor development of children up to the age of 7 years which included a study of the Australian Fundamental Motor Skills Programme (Department of Education, Victoria 1996), as an example of a system for use in the analysis of gross motor skills. They watched the video and used the handbook to gain knowledge and understanding of motor skill acquisition and of detailed analysis of a range of activities. They worked together in a practical session on peer observation and analysis of some of the activities seen on video and prepared to try out selected activities in school with children aged 5 and 6 years. Following the teaching session, during which they worked in pairs, observing and making field notes on a child, they attempted a diagnostic analysis of the child's achievements from their observations and notes.

For example, the guidance offered in the manual to assist in analysing the forehand strike included focus of the eyes, standing side-on to the target, stepping towards target with the opposite foot to the striking arm during strike and following through towards the target. One of the students, Emma, reported on her pupil, Rosie (aged 6), as follows:

> Rosie's forehand strike was better than the level stipulated for a child of her age. Not only did she keep her eyes focused on the ball throughout the strike but she also could be seen stepping towards the ball with the opposite foot to her striking arm. After a few attempts Rosie realised that if she followed through towards the target she would give her strike more power.

About James' catching, his trainee teacher noted:

> James stood about 7 metres away from the feeder. He kept his eyes focused on the ball throughout, prepared his arms, elbows and hands correctly and moved his hands to meet the ball competently each time. After further conversation and example, he realised that bringing the ball in towards his chest secured it more firmly.

Assessment

Hayes (1999: 5, 6) suggests that teachers need to take account of all the facts before drawing conclusions, then to use an appropriate assessment technique, to make formative assessments as they note children's responses, listen, discuss, look at output and then to assess before offering advice, giving an opinion, explaining new possibilities or showing that something is wrong. They should monitor, to weigh up the position and to intervene as appropriate.

The trainees described above attempted to try out all of this advice and they also studied the Attainment Target for Physical Education in the National Curriculum (DfEE 1999), noting the descriptors for each of levels 1, 2 and 3. The attainment target sets out the knowledge, skills and understanding which pupils of different abilities and maturities are expected to have by the end of each key stage.

In physical education, levels 1–3 include:

- skill acquisition
- development of coordination and control
- movement memory
- linking and sequencing
- planning and evaluating performance
- tactics and compositional ideas
- safety
- exercise and health.

Having worked with their pupil, they then attempted to write a report, based on the work achieved in the one session, as feedback for the children's teacher. Emma wrote of Rosie:

> Rosie was very confident in her own ability. She attempted a number of different activities with maturity and enthusiasm. She was able to explore simple skills, while repeating, copying and remembering the skill pointers we taught her. Rosie was mature in her response and understanding of her peer's performance. It was clear that she was able to observe her peers and see ways to improve her own performance. She was able to vary her responses to the tasks according to individual situations. I would suggest that Rosie is a level 2, working well towards level 3 in all that she did with us.

Of Maxwell (aged 6), his trainee teacher, Iona, reported:

> Maxwell's skills seem to match the level 2 requirements. He was able to copy, remember and repeat the actions demonstrated by us. He had very good control and coordination overall. He had his own ideas about the techniques involved within these skills and was able to explain these clearly. He suggested ways in which he could improve. He was very cooperative and we really enjoyed working with him.

The report on James (aged 6), by his trainee teacher, Joanna, reads:

> James was competent in almost all the activities. He was especially good at catching/throwing and batting the ball, also kicking. He was consistently accurate in receiving the ball and was capable of comparing his own performance with given examples and correctly improving his own. He was not so capable at leaping, where he found it difficult to land on one foot. James talked about his enthusiasm for

tennis. I think James is probably at level 2, capable of repeating activities with control and coordination. He was able to improve his skill by observing others. He enjoyed the activities and I think he is very capable for his age.

Joanna has obviously made the most of the available time with James, giving him a wide range of experiences from which she learnt much from her observation and interaction about his all-round knowledge and performance.

The trainees were learning to level children as a means of ascertaining current achievement, in order to extend the children's opportunities, to raise standards and as benchmarks to ensure effective learning and teaching. They also attempted to relate the children to the levels provided in the Attainment Target for Physical Education in the National Curriculum (DfEE 1999), in order to inform the class teacher. For the class teacher, this was an opportunity not only to observe her class at work with other teachers, but also to gain detailed feedback on each child's performance, participation and potential.

Reporting

The *Assessment and Reporting Arrangements 2000* (QCA 1999c) state that the principles of good report writing include the importance of writing in a clear and straightforward way, targeting the audience and indicating how the child is performing in relation to their potential and past achievements, as well as in relation to the rest of the class. Noting the child's strengths and achievements as well as areas for development and improvement are cited, along with whether the child is happy, settled and behaving well. Focusing on learning and motivating the child to make further progress are further qualities of successful reports. The example given in the QCA document for a school report on an 11-year-old child in physical education indicates that for each aspect achieved, there was yet more to accomplish. For example, it suggests that, in dance, the child created interesting sequences, but found it difficult to remember them, and in games was well coordinated, but needed to develop tactical skills.

The trainees' report writing as outlined above shows a keen awareness of many of the issues pertaining to effective reporting. They are able to record successes, they also look more broadly than on performance only, they are sensitive to the children's ability to evaluate their own performance, to observe, to practise and improve and to demonstrate their knowledge and under-standing of the activities being learnt. The writing is supportive of the learner. At this early stage in their training these trainee teachers have shown very good potential for effective reporting and went on to learn about target-setting, for prompting further achievements of their pupils.

Contexts for observation and assessment

In order to maintain continuous knowledge of each child, High/ Scope recommends the regular observation, assessment and not-ing of each child's progress. Many of the themes of observation of the pre-school child which High/Scope includes are essentially movement related. This neatly demonstrates the importance of motor competence for success in a wide range of other develop-mental activities. The following are the developmental themes used in High/Scope, with examples of some of their movement-dependent dimensions.

- Creative Representation, including recognizing objects by touch, making models, role playing, drawing and painting
- Language and Literacy, including writing
- Social Relations/Initiative, including collaborative play, taking care of one's own needs
- Music, including playing instruments
- Classification, including sorting and matching
- Seriation, including arranging objects in order
- Space, including filling and emptying, fitting things together and taking them apart, folding, twisting, stretching and stacking things, experiencing relative positions in play space, building, neighbourhood
- Time, including starting and stopping actions, rates of move-ment, experiencing time intervals, experiencing sequence of events.

The theme of movement incorporates a range of movement-related activities, focusing on moving in place and from place to place, moving with objects, expressing creativity, expressing beat and moving with others. The only theme which does not specifically state a movement dimension is that of Number, but even here, it is easy to see the value of competent movement ability, for example, in handling blocks or counters for basic number activities. Dexterity in picking up and managing equipment is an essential motor skill for mathematics. In England, the foundation stage of education commences when children reach the age of 3 and the *Early Learning Goals* (QCA 1999a) set out what children should have achieved by the end of the reception year, at the age of 5 years. Areas of learning are defined which include personal, social and emotional development; language and literacy; mathematical development; knowledge and understanding of the world; physical development and creative development. As with High/Scope, many of the *Early Learning Goals* are dependent upon motor competence, indeed 14 of the 15 illustrations in the document are of children engaged in either gross or fine motor activity. In Cameo 2, the teacher addresses the importance of proficient fine motor functioning through providing regular practice sessions, with coaching for her children, while she also observes and assesses development. She includes familiar activities, such as cutting, painting, drawing, sorting, keyboard, and also introduces less familiar tasks, to see how well children handle and adapt to new situations. Brett (aged 4) was working with Plasticine for his cutting activity. He coped very well with scissors when cutting Plasticine whereas in a later activity, cutting paper was not as easy for him. Note that in Figure 4.14 he uses the scissors in his right hand, whereas when fitting legs on to his monster he uses his left hand (see Figure 1.3).

Another context for observation and assessment in England is the National Curriculum for Physical Education (in DfEE 1999), which sets out an attainment target and describes the knowledge, skills and understanding which children should have achieved by the end of each key stage. Each attainment target consists of eight level descriptions as well as a description for exceptional performance. These levels are not intended to be a description of the curriculum, but should mainly be used at the end of each key stage, to provide the basis for deciding each child's attainment. It is suggested that children in Key Stage 1 will work within levels 1 to 3, with the majority achieving level 2 by the age of 7. It is suggested that children should be able to 'copy, repeat and explore simple skills and actions with basic control and coordination' at level 1. This nicely builds from the

Figure 4.14 Brett (aged 3) cutting legs for his monster

Early Learning Goals for Physical Development (DfEE 2000), which refer to moving with confidence, control and coordination, with awareness of space and self'. Subsequent levels call for the ability to remember actions learnt, to vary skills, to select and use skills and actions appropriately and to apply them with coordination and control in a range of situations.

While the instruction to teachers in applying the levels is to 'judge which description best fits the pupil's performance', in the case of physical education, the term 'performance' here refers to more than just the 'doing' of PE. The Programme of Study provides for children to acquire and develop skills, to select and apply skills and compositional ideas, to evaluate and improve performance and to acquire knowledge and understanding of fitness and health. The level descriptions, therefore, incorporate all four of these elements, in striving to produce not only performers, but also children with a broad and balanced physical education who are able not only to describe what they know, but also to select and apply, to evaluate and analyse and to demonstrate knowledge and understanding. In my childhood, PE was about doing, about copying the teacher, about striving to do it better and about working in silence. The physical education learning environment of the twenty-first century is interactional and educational, in addition to offering the 'training' opportunities that were the hallmark of the middle of the twentieth century.

Use of information and communications technology (ICT)

Methods of recording observation in order to assess and set targets for further development are set to be transformed in the twenty-first century, through the use of ICT for observation of movement to aid assessment and the provision of feedback to enhance learning. Schools can now use video to demonstrate examples of good practice for children to watch and copy. The video camera can also be used to record movement, with the added bonuses of providing almost immediate feedback as well as feedback that can be reviewed repeatedly, as needed. Instant feedback is known to be an essential criterion for potential improvement in movement development as is the opportunity to review the feedback several times, thereby facilitating detailed attention to elements of the performance.

'Oh, yes, I can see it now!' How often have children expressed this revelation when watching their performance on video, having not been able to make use of the accurate and repeated oral feedback of their teacher? Seeing is believing and seeing can so speedily lead to understanding and improvement.

Additionally, the use of digital photography can bring still photos into feedback on performance, and the use of interactive CD-ROM with large screen make for easily observed points of reference for large numbers of pupils at one time. Not only is ICT brilliant for teaching observation and for providing accurate feedback, but also children can use ICT for keeping their own records of achievement, for maintaining checklists of achievements and record sheets, such as that exemplified in the *Gym Kit Handbook* (Maude 1994; see also Figure 4.15).

A number of other writers summarize assessment in the following ways. Assessment is 'at the very heart of the process of promoting children's learning' (Raymond 1998: 169) and is also 'a key to learning' (David 1999: 32). Raymond (1998: 176) assesses children in physical education by talking to them individually or in groups as they work or reflect on work and by listening carefully to what they say as they discuss tasks set or as they evaluate their own work or the work of others.

Hayes (1999: 6) claims that assessment is integral to planning

Gymnastics
Assessment

Key Stage 2

Name of child:

Element	Statement
Sustaining physical activity	
Knowledge and performance of gymnastic actions	
Sequencing ability	
Use of apparatus	
Safe practice	
Action Plan	

Figure 4.15 Key Stage 2 (aged 7–11 years) gymnastics assessment

and teaching. It is essential to establish what is already known and use assessment constructively to monitor learning and to create opportunities. Assessment is useful only if it assists the pupils' understanding, promotes a keener interest in the work and is accompanied by appropriate support in the form of advice, guidance or explanation. It is also important to take note of what pupils' achievements tell you about your own teaching methods and effectiveness. He goes on to warn that assessment does not always improve learning: 'Unless assessment and recording have a positive impact on teaching effectiveness, you may as well save yourself the trouble' (Hayes 1999: 85).

The School Examination and Assessment Council (1991: 11) suggests that: 'Pupils can be actively involved in their own assessment: reviewing their work and progress; setting targets for learning; and deciding in discussion with teachers, which pieces of work provide evidence of particular attainment.'

Hayes (1999: 5, 6) suggests that we need to take account of all the facts before drawing conclusions, to use an appropriate assessment technique, to make formative assessments as we note children's responses, listen, discuss, look at output and then assess before offering advice, giving an opinion, explaining new possibilities or to show that something is wrong. We need to monitor, to weigh up the position and to intervene as appropriate.

The purposes of assessment, then, are to

- determine children's progress, achievements, strengths, weaknesses and needs
- assist learning
- provide progression
- raise standards of pupil achievement, motivation and behaviour.

Assessment should

- form a natural part of teaching and learning
- arise from current classroom practice
- build upon a child's previous experience
- match the child's abilities
- be a shared process with the child who needs to know what is expected and why the learning environment is structured in specific ways
- involve the child who should be challenged to reflect critically on learning in terms of the process involved and the product achieved
- focus on the extent to which the learning outcomes match the curricular intentions.

(Raymond 1998: 170)

It is worth noting advice from the Hereford and Worcester County Council (1992: 51) *Physical Education Guidelines*, which suggest that:

- not everything you teach needs to be assessed
- not everything you assess needs to be recorded
- not everything you record needs to be reported.

Summary

Drummond (1993: 97) suggests that 'Assessment is essentially provisional, partial, tentative, exploratory and invariably incomplete. It is not an end in itself, but a means to an end.' Assessment is just a tool, a very powerful tool, for use in the provision of both 'feedback' and 'feed forward' (DES Task Group on Assessment and Testing 1988: 35) to enhance children's learning and achievement. The role of effective assessment is a process in which our understanding of children's learning, acquired through observation and reflection, can also be used to evaluate and enrich the curriculum we offer.

Questions to ask

1 How can we help children to develop their observation skills in order to improve their movement learning?
2 Is there need for greater provision for children of self and peer assessment and for peer tutoring to enhance movement learning? If so, how can these be introduced and developed?
3 What are the most effective assessment strategies to adopt in your school, class or setting to ensure that each child progresses at the most appropriate pace towards being physically literate?

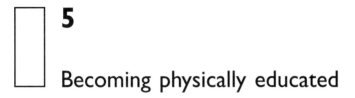

5

Becoming physically educated

Cameo 1
In his final year at primary school, Daniel (aged 11) is writing his physical education profile, to *send* to his new PE teacher in his secondary school. He is proud of being able to swim 100 metres, he can play all three types of games and has high scores in his primary school's athletics challenge. In gym he especially enjoys sequences on apparatus and can do forward and backward rolls, cartwheels and handstands. He took part in the class dance performance and has asked if his new teacher will see the video. He hopes that there will be outdoor and adventurous activities at the new school because he loves orienteering and belongs to the local club with his family.

Cameo 2
Charlotte (aged 6) is exploring the apparatus, learning to use her hands and feet to go up, down and through the climbing frame smoothly and to go on, off, along and over the benches quickly and lightly. She also knows how to jump and land, to balance and to roll with confidence and she loves doing gym because it is exciting and you are always learning something new.

Introduction

In this chapter we explore first a range of contexts in which children can access opportunities to become physically educated, including the historical context, the context of the school curriculum, the extra-curricular programme in school and within partnerships, including partner schools, home and community. Second, we consider the child as a learner, getting to know what it is to be physically educated, to gain knowledge and success as a dancer, gymnast and games player who also learns the skills of athletics, swimming and outdoor and adventurous activities, while still in primary school. Finally the role of the teacher is discussed, in delivering and facilitating these experiences and learning, with suggestions from recent developments of ways of ensuring an even better physical education for the children of the twenty-first century.

The context

Historical context

The quality of physical education today is partly a product of the movement learning experiences of our predecessors. Interestingly, history provides a forward-looking context for our aspirations for the new century, that all children have an entitlement to become physically educated.

Way back in 700 BC, gymnastics and athletics were the skills that enabled the physically educated to participate in the Olympic Games, whereas education in the Minoan period in Crete required the learner to be articulate in acrobatics! There were two components to becoming an educated person among the early Greeks, namely music and bodily exercise. Moving rapidly to the twentieth century and to Britain rather than Greece, the 1933 *Syllabus for Physical Training* (Board of Education 1933) included among its principal teaching aims for young children: to achieve lightness and spring, body flexibility and the securing of good health; to encourage alertness and a bright, happy, fearless independent spirit. Also included were posture, rhythm and the rudiments of fair play in games and the 1933 Syllabus was carefully structured to provide careful progression according to children's developmental sequence. For example, one of the 'primary objects of physical training is to show how correct positions of the body in sitting, standing and in the ordinary activities of daily life may become habitual' (Board of Education 1933: 12). This was taught

Figure 5.1   Correct standing posture in 1933

on a daily basis, from the start of schooling. The command 'Attention' was not to be introduced until the junior school because of the physical and mental demands that it required, over and above the ability to assume the correct standing posture (Figure 5.1; see Board of Education 1933: 87).

The system of Swedish gymnastics was introduced in the UK in the early 1900s. This led to the daily drill exercises within the 1933 Syllabus which children experienced in British primary schools up to the 1940s. Almost 10 years later, the Ministry of Education (1952), in its publication *Planning the Programme*, stated that physical education in the primary school should be about activity, skill, versatility and quality. The rigidity and seemingly military approach of the 1933 syllabus then began to give way to a more educational approach in which the intellect, as well as the body were exposed to learning. By 1972 the Department of Education and Science (DES) saw movement education as a two-way channel of learning, both as a way of finding out and as a form of accomplishment. This double focus for teaching and learning must surely be a key aspiration for all time, catering as it does both for the process, or ongoing developmental stages and the product, or the final piece of completed work. It also incorporates both intellectual development and performance development. By 1988, the Education Reform Act (ERA) seemed to offer an apparently secure and exciting future for physical education with the inclusion of PE as a compulsory subject throughout the 5–16 curriculum.

In 1990 the Interim Report of the DES National Curriculum Physical Education Working Group opens with the statement: 'Physical Education is the only subject which, through the use and knowledge of the body and its movement, contributes to *all* aspects of the education of young people' (DES 1990: 5).

Physical education, the report continues:

- develops physical competence
- promotes physical development
- teaches pupils, through experience, to know about and value the benefits of exercise
- establishes self-esteem through the development of physical confidence
- develops artistic and aesthetic understanding within and through movement
- helps pupils to cope with both success and failure in the context of cooperative and competitive physical activities
- provides experience of physical activities which should lead pupils to lifelong participation
- contributes to the development of problem-solving skills, inter-personal skills and the forging of links between the school and the community, and across cultures.

It was proposed that the three-fold attainment targets for PE should be planning and composing, participating and performing, appreciating and evaluating. This was the first appearance of progressive statements of attainment which provided not only for the physical aspects of PE, but also for the knowledge and understanding aspects of PE, contained in the prescribed curriculum.

By 1995, the target of raising standards, contained in the Education Reform Act, encouraged curriculum planners to make proposals for new approaches to games teaching, for the introduction of health-related exercise initiatives and for enhancing the curriculum in athletics, dance, gymnastics, outdoor and adventurous activities and swimming. The sum of these opportunities constituted the potential for a broad, balanced physical education curriculum. Interestingly, the 1933 syllabus also included several teaching aims related to healthy exercise:

- to maintain flexibility of body and so prevent or reduce the need for corrective exercises in later years

- to stimulate respiration and circulation by encouraging free activity, so aiding growth and helping to secure good health.

These aims are now emerging again, even more strongly than before, alongside the challenge to each citizen to take personal responsibility for the maintenance of a healthy and active lifestyle. Inactivity-induced illness was seen as a malaise of the late twentieth century and children were seen as being particularly at risk. This risk came about by the reduction in PE time in primary schools due to the overcrowded curriculum, to children increasingly travelling to school by car, rather than on foot or by bike, and to the dominance of television and computers in recreational time rather than outdoor play.

School context

Curriculum 2000 for Physical Education in England (DfEE 1999) claims the importance of physical education as the development of physical competence and confidence and the ability to use these to perform in a range of activities. The curriculum addresses knowledge and understanding as well as the skills and performance aspects of physical education, which is an important emphasis, since to be physically educated is to know more than just the doing aspects of PE. Indeed, knowledge and understanding are fundamental to successful skill acquisition, to movement development and to competent performance of PE activities. Knowledge and understanding are also implicit elements of the physical education attainment target, which includes the selection and application of skills, in tactics and compositional ideas, the evaluation and improvement of performance and learning about fitness and health.

The physical education curriculum in England is designed to offer a broad and balanced learning experience for all children and draws on six main types of activities, namely dance, games and gymnastics from the start of their schooling and also athletics, outdoor and adventurous activities (O and AA) and swimming. Each of these activities has its own language, social construct and emotional tone (Douglas 1999: 2). Each of these activities is made up of discrete content as well as cross-activity content through which children can make transfers of learning and can apply experience from one activity to another. For example,

landing safely from jumping on the floor in dance can be effectively applied to landing from jumping on to and jumping from
apparatus in gymnastics. Landing safely in the athletic events
of high and long jump and in daily life such as landing from
jumping off the bottom stair, or from rock to rock on the beach,
can also be applied to landing safely from jumping off the bus.
Transfers of learning can be applied to less predictable situations
such as in intercepting a pass in basketball, negotiating unfamiliar
obstacles in O and AA and in managing a myriad of movement
challenges of daily life.

While the curriculum offered great opportunities for children
to be physically educated in the primary school, the new millennium dawned with a concern at UK ministerial level that 40 per
cent of primary schools had reported that PE provision had significantly decreased and that 90 per cent of primary schools had
no gym, swimming pool or hard play area (as reported in the
Guardian, 11 January 2000, 'Ofsted inspectors target school sports
to find a new generation of athletes'). The British government
has determined to target facilities and time in an attempt to raise
standards in physical education, with a view to raising levels of
sporting achievement.

Partnership contexts

The playscheme described in Chapter 2 involved local firms as
sponsor partners for the purchase of equipment, storage sheds
and training opportunities for adult and pupil play leaders. The
club continues to benefit from sponsorship, for the maintenance
of consumable equipment. Membership of the club is open to all
pupils, so that everyone can participate in fulfilling a number of
important personal and educational aims, the first of which is:

• promoting improved levels of health and fitness in all pupils.

To the visitor, the overall impression is of high levels of activity
in designated areas of the infant and junior playgrounds that have
been specially designed to cater for group and individual activities
of both high intensity and lower intensity activity (Figure 5.2).
For example, hoppers and skippers predominate on one side,
while bats, balls and duck walkers occupy another and a third
area abounds in toy vehicles, touring the marked roads, catering
for a wide range of interests and providing for both gross and

Figure 5.2   General view of an active playground

fine motor activity and practice and to enhance physical education (Figures 5.3 and 5.4).

- developing a sense of citizenship through developing positive attitudes, behaviour and teamwork

Older pupils were invited to apply for specific jobs of their choice, including helping younger children to play and enabling older children's mini-games by refereeing and timing small-sided games such as football and basketball. They were also responsible for managing the loans of equipment.

- developing a love of games activities and sporting skills
- providing a structure to the lunch break resulting in the overall enhancement of children's learning and physical education.

The Umbrella Association in a Cambridgeshire village community provides for a range of after-school and weekend activities for children as well as adults. Among the PE-related activities for children are gymnastics, swimming and football.

Figure 5.3   We get puffed out on the hoppers!

Figure 5.4   I'm getting better on stilts (Lucy, aged 11)

Raising standards in physical education was a key objective for primary schools in the late 1990s, even though the educational climate in schools called for seriously large concentrations of time, teaching and resources to be allocated to literacy and numeracy. In the face of this, one of the highly successful outcomes of the National Lottery in England was the channelling of funding into school sport through the setting up of the Youth Sport Trust (YST) to work in partnership with local education authorities and primary schools. The Youth Sport Trust was provided with Lottery funding to set up the 'TOP' initiative, with the aim of helping to increase children's participation in sport. This funding was used to inject new opportunities into school sport with the provision of equipment and resources into schools along with training for whole schools staff. The provision was intended to assist in developing both the physical education curriculum and extra-curricular sport.

The scheme commenced with 'TOP Play 'for children aged 5–9 and 'TOP Sport' for children between the ages of 7 and 11. The teaching and learning in TOP Play is about sport skills and about working alone and in pairs on introductory games-playing strategies related to the three main types of games, namely 'invasion', 'net-wall' and 'strike-field' (Figure 5.5).

TOP Sport builds on this firm foundation and consists of resources and equipment for named games, from each of the three games types, such as basketball, tennis and cricket, along with inservice courses for teachers, all at no cost to the school (Figure 5.6). One of the aims of the YST was to train sufficient appropriate trainers all over the UK so that every primary teacher would be TOP trained in four years.

Although the TOP scheme was originally a games-orientated initiative, it soon expanded to include 'TOP' Gymnastics, Athletics, Outdoors, Swimming, Dance and 'Fit for TOP'.

Partnerships with home and with early years settings were also included in the TOP scheme through the launch of 'TOP Tots' and 'TOP Start'. These schemes offer parents, carers and practitioners ideas for extending young children's motor skill experiences and development. The colourful, attractive and interesting equipment supplied with the scheme is immediately attractive to young players. This early targeting of children's physical education was a significant addition to early years provision at the turn of the century. The impact of the TOP scheme

Figure 5.5 TOP Play in action

has been very significant in raising awareness at both government and local level of the need to enhance children's skill levels, to give time and commitment to physical education and to review the provision of opportunities for children to participate in worthwhile physical activity, within and outside the curriculum. Two further developments by the Youth Sport Trust have been first a commitment to inclusion, particularly for children with disabilities, and second the introduction of the 'TOP-up' scheme which provides resources and staff training as support for those who offer extra-curricular activities in schools. As the impact of the Youth Sport Trust grows, so will its influence on schools' curricular and extra-curricular physical education as well as assisting in community provision of sport and recreation.

The contexts in which children can become physically educated include:

Figure 5.6 TOP Sport in action

- environments, equipment and resources within and outside the school, designed for the physical education of the modern child
- the curriculum with all its rich past and current breadth and depth of opportunities
- time, seemingly the scarcest resource and yet the most valuable for the embedding of physical education experience and knowledge
- national and local schemes and partnerships to extend children's physical education opportunities.

The child

What is it for children to be physically educated in the primary school? What should they expect as their entitlement, how should they go about accessing this and what should they expect to take with them into their secondary schooling by way of skills, performance ability, knowledge and understanding? The National Curriculum for Physical Education in England, produced for the year 2000, provides answers to some of these questions. The activities to be studied are dance, games and gymnastics for all primary school age children, with athletics, outdoor and adventurous activities and swimming for children of junior age. This broad curriculum provides a wide range of activities and each activity in the PE curriculum offers unique learning opportunities and challenges for all children.

Dance

Gardner (1993a: 223) states that, 'of all the uses of the body, none has reached greater heights than the dance'. 'Everybody dances!' states Peter Brinson (1991: 1). He claims that the secret of the continuing influence of dance is the 'power of movement to express inner feelings and outside experiences which cannot be expressed in words' (Brinson 1993: 3). Dance in Britain, he suggested, 'embraces every kind of movement invention', from jazz to ballet, ballroom to disco, traditional dances of the British Isles to international and historical dance. 'Dance has the power to illuminate wide aspects of our lives.'

This is corroborated by Lord Palumbo, who says: 'Dance is a popular social activity, a prime means of expressing cultural heritage and identity, a dynamic and continually changing art. It is part of the cultural fabric of contemporary life' (Arts Council 1993: 1). What should children expect from their dance education? By the end of their primary school education they should have explored and engaged in, and gained knowledge and understanding of, the vocabulary of dance, including travel, turn, jump, gesture, pause and stillness. They should know how to incorporate changes in body shape, speed, direction and level into dances. Dance education should also include enhancement of young

Figure 5.7 Amanda's spikey jump

children's developing movement patterns. As they gain experience, dance should include creating and performing dances and learning about choreography, as well as enabling children to develop their ability to express and communicate personal ideas and feelings through dance. Exploring rhythm in dance links neatly with learning about rhythm in music, as does the possibility of responding to a range of stimuli and accompaniments in dance as well as in music.

Look at the gesture and vigour incorporated into Amanda's jump (Figure 5.7) when she was just 7 years old. How often do we find a child so well coordinated at such a young age, and so capable of achieving an articulate and dynamic asymmetrical shape, with such skilful coordination. She thoroughly enjoyed dance in her primary school because she was free to choose how she wanted to express her feelings. Although Amanda also became an excellent gymnast and games player and later went on to

Figure 5.8 We can dance the maypole

captain her university in cricket, she always remembered her dance experience with great joy and a sense of accomplishment. Those who taught her remember her ability to communicate 'aesthetic value' (Gardner 1993a: 223), one of the criteria for successful dance performance.

The dance curriculum should include dances from within our own culture and across cultures, from our own country and from distant locations as well as the latest popular dances and dances from past times. By way of contrast with Amanda's experience, the children in Figure 5.8 are proud of their skill in maypole dancing. They have quite a reputation locally for plaiting and unplaiting the maypole without a single knot or mistake. They can talk about their success at dipping and diving and they also know the rhythms of the dance and just how much 'puff' is needed to keep on skipping throughout the dance and to stay in time with the other dancers. How old are they? They are mostly 6 years old and are in their final year in an inner city infant school. They also know the number work involved in plaiting the maypole, how many moves to count and the numbers to be remembered at each stage of the dance. Their teacher knows that once the dance starts, the dancers will not need to be prompted and will, almost certainly, plait the ribbons around the pole and unplait them successfully and end their dance with the ending of the music.

Gymnastics

Gymnastics is about mastery of the body. Young children run, jump, climb, roll and scramble over obstacles for sheer joy. As they grow older, increasing skill leads them to try 'unpredictable antics of their own invention and to do impossible things in impossible ways' (DES 1972: 25). Mastering the skills of gymnastics such as locomotion, flight and balance involves strength, stamina and flexibility to bend, extend, twist and turn the body with control, coordination, resilience and fluency, while working on the floor and meeting the challenges of the apparatus. Gymnastics gives

Figure 5.9   I enjoy being in the air

Figure 5.10 Peter (aged 6) makes a strong shape in gymnastics

scope for ingenuity, versatility and adaptability as well as efficient body management, agility, acrobatics and creativity.

Charlotte in Cameo 2 (at the start of the chapter) increases her knowledge of locomotion skills to negotiate the bench and calls on her prior knowledge of the crawling action of the hands and feet, using her skills, strength and courage to scale the heights, negotiating the climbing apparatus safely and with fluency. Gymnastics also involves children in the movement vocabulary associated with being upside-down, in rolling, cartwheeling and handstanding activities and with negotiating obstacles in the environment safely and efficiently. Gymnastics helps them to focus on health-related matters such as the importance of developing strength in the arms, shoulders, legs and body, and of maintaining and improving flexibility, particularly in the wrists, shoulders, spine, ankles and hips. For children who work hard in gym, travelling energetically, and spending more time in the air than on the floor, there is also the profit to be gained of increasing stamina (Figure 5.9).

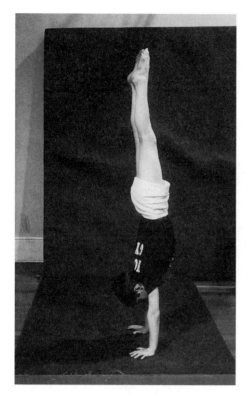

Figure 5.11 Theo (aged 9) balancing upside-down on the floor

In Figure 5.10, Peter is working hard to improve his stamina, strength and flexibility as he holds this balance on his hands.

Balancing is an important element of the gymnastics curriculum, which, when practised alongside travelling, offers a challenging contrast of activities, from stillness to moving, from the body tension created in order to hold the body weight in balances, to the controlled freedom of travelling through the space around and above (Figure 5.11).

While both gymnastics and dance should comprise expressive movement, gymnastics also provides for concentration on objective, functional movement, demanding technical accuracy. Whereas dance involves the use of gesture to express mood and feeling, as demonstrated by Amanda, both gymnastics and dance call for choreographic learning and movement memory, in the

Figure 5.12 A pair and group balance in gymnastics

linking of movements to create phrases and then sequences of movement. In both activities, learners have the opportunity to work alone and to manage their own movement within the space shared with all the other children in the class. Both activities also teach children to work with a partner and in groups. The maypole dance is an example of a group dance and the pairs and trio balances in Figure 5.12 are examples of close and accurate cooperation in gymnastics.

Games

Games are the most traditional and most practised of all children's physical education activities. Games were often formerly associated with the 'playing fields of Eton' and games teaching in the past often concentrated almost exclusively on team games such as hockey, which are known as invasion games. These are the games in which one team invades the playing space of the other team to score goals in the opponents' half of the playing area. Such games include the British national sport of football as well as rugby, netball, basketball, hockey and lacrosse. These games, when played

Figure 5.13   I want to learn about tennis (Julie, aged 5)

well, offer great opportunities for team participation, for much exercise through running about and for great pleasure and a sense of achievement. While invasion games offer an excellent learning experience for some children, they do not meet the needs of all and are just a part of the whole games curriculum. Thus, the current games curriculum in primary schools offers a broader and more balanced approach to games and includes all three of the games types. These are net games, strike and field games and invasion games. Examples of net games are tennis, badminton and volleyball and examples of strike and field games are cricket, rounders and baseball. Two important educational improvements in children's games experience today are that the equipment available for schools is designed for children, to suit the size and strength of younger players, while the games areas, rules and numbers of players in teams are appropriately designed and devised to suit the age and experience of the players. Thus Short tennis, Quick Cricket and Unihoc have superseded the adult versions, with appropriately smaller playing areas, child-friendly equipment and small numbers on each team, thereby giving a greater number of children more opportunities for more active participation throughout the game (Figure 5.13). Such strategies should lead to greater success in learning to play and enjoy games for all children.

Figure 5.14   Two-in-a-team rounders

Games learning in the primary school focuses on developing the skills necessary to participate in game-related activities, working alone, in pairs and in small groups. Through these activities children learn techniques and game strategies such as the principles of attack and defence and the tactics needed when more experienced, to play full-scale games. For example, in developing the game of rounders, a teacher started with the children working alone, learning to control the ball and a range of bats of different shapes and sizes. From there they practised bowling and hitting in pairs, at first using bats with a flat face and a soft ball, taking turns to bowl and hit. Both children ran to follow the ball after each hit, playing freely in a large space. They learnt to make their own decisions about which equipment was most appropriate and about the best distance between bowler and batter. They knew that as they got better they should try to get further away from each other. The next progression was for two pairs to play against one another, with one team made up of bowler and batter, while the other pair worked together as the fielders (Figure 5.14). After each child had bowled and batted once, the teams changed over. Runs were scored by the batter running between two markers, while the fielders collected and returned the ball and the bowler kept the score of the batter's runs. Batters were encouraged to run whether or not they had hit the ball. Fielders were encouraged to play as a team, running to cover the distance back to the bowling area and passing the ball between them. The bowler, being on the same team as the batter, was motivated to bowl 'good' balls for their partner to hit, thus offering maximum opportunity for success to the batter. Through this series of progressions children were given maximum opportunity for achievement of success at each stage and in each role, and learnt the benefits of close cooperation between one another to achieve success in playing as a team.

Athletics

By the time children go on to secondary school they will be familiar with the basic athletic skills of running, jumping and throwing and will have learnt about the techniques of some athletics events, within a wide-ranging curriculum of athletic activities such as is promoted in the TOP programme and the Athletics Association's Ten Step scheme. These schemes include additional athletics-related activities such as compass run and shuttle run, which can enhance sprinting skills without the need to race over specific, linear distances. Whereas only one child at a time can be practising long jump into a sand landing area, many children can learn techniques of jumping, by practising standing long jump or hop, step and jump along a safe grassy area. If this area is also marked with metre and 25 centimetre lines children can measure or estimate their achievements, by comparing their point of landing to the metre and centimetre lines marked. Alternatively a measuring tape can be extended through the centre of the area and each child can check the point of landing by walking across to see their achievement against the tape. Maximum participation and practice are fundamental to building up the skills, strength and stamina essential for competence in athletics.

Outdoor and adventurous activities

Here children learn how to participate in and meet the demands of outdoor activities, including following trails in familiar, unfamiliar and changing environments. They experience the skills involved in participating competently and safely in challenging activities, avoiding danger and minimizing risk. They learn about orienteering and problem-solving activities and how to cooperate with others to meet and overcome challenges. Outdoor and adventurous activities demand physical competence, fitness, judgement and application of knowledge. They are also a fundamental way of developing an appreciation of, awareness of and caring attitude towards the environment, through observation and interpretation of the immediate physical and social environment. This aspect of PE also provides a vital link to the ideal of lifelong learning and health. For younger children such activities may at first be practised within the safety of the school hall, or immediate outdoor areas of the school playground and grass areas. With experience and maturity O & AA may be learnt away from the school site, perhaps in a park, forest or at the coast. Many schools include O & AA learning during residential experiences.

Swimming activities and water safety

'Swimming is an essential part of every child's physical education' (Elkington 1998: 1). She sees swimming as a fundamental life skill which is also a prerequisite for water-based activities such as sailing, canoeing or water skiing. Swimming develops self-reliance, independence and judgement. Teaching a class of beginners is one of the most stimulating and rewarding challenges for a teacher! Seeing the speed with which most children achieve confidence in the water, through fun activities which develop movement, buoyancy, flotation and propulsion, is most exciting. One of the great milestones in children's physical education achievements is knowing that you have swum, that you have achieved those first swimming strokes, with both arms and legs helping and not even a toe on the ground! That every child should be able to swim a distance of at least 25 metres by the age of 11 years is a statutory requirement in England. In addition to becoming competent swimmers with recognizable stroke techniques such as breast stroke, front crawl and back crawl, the curriculum includes activities and skills such as sculling, floating and surface diving. Meeting challenges related to speed, distance and personal survival are also part of the learning as are the safety, health and fitness aspects of swimming.

Becoming physically educated, however, is more than the sum of the parts of the statutory PE programme. Daniel in Cameo 1 had achieved much in his primary school, was proud of those achievements and was confident in his physical education. He had gained wide experience of the statutory curriculum and knew what he had learnt. He was articulate in the movement vocabulary of PE as well as articulate in using the language of physical education to communicate his knowledge. He participated fully in every aspect of PE and was also highly motivated towards further learning, an important factor in future success, specially at the point of changing schools. At this stage in his education his teacher agreed that he was physically educated. Children who are proud of their progress in PE in school, who 'have a go' at everything, enjoy their teachers' lessons, know what they are learning about, work to their full potential, learn from observation and know what they have achieved, stand a very good chance of becoming physically educated. Physically educated children are also confident, independent, mature and articulate in language and movement and in the ways that they manage their learning, the organization and the safety aspects of PE and are able to follow up preferences and specialisms in school and community clubs.

The teacher

Providing the teaching necessary to support all aspects of children's physical literacy calls not only for knowledge and understanding of children's physical and movement development, but also knowledge of physical education and of teaching styles appropriate for effective learning. Ofsted (1995: 1) characterized high quality teaching in primary physical education as including:

- high expectations of levels of achievement
- effective planning and organization of lessons
- acute observation skills
- clear feedback
- good judgement of when to intervene in the learning process
- communication of enthusiasm and promotion of positive attitudes participation, to competition, sportsmanship and fair play
- evidence of engaging in staff development.

Also cited were schools with sound policies and curriculum plans, equality of opportunity for pupils, effective assessment, recording and reporting practices.

The foundation stage (age 3–5 years)

Practitioners and carers have a crucial role to play in the success of children's early physical education experience, through supporting their acquisition of mature movement patterns in fundamental movement skills, and also in the whole range of gross and fine motor skills. Research has emphasized the importance of motor activity in the development of pathways in the brain which promote learning (Wetton 1999: 3). Teachers also know that gross motor skill precedes fine motor skill and that if a child has not yet mastered the balance and management of their own body it would be too much to expect that child to sit down and engage in the fine motor skills associated, for example, with the current literacy and numeracy programmes.

Guidance from the Department of Education, Victoria (1996) proved very helpful to trainee teachers in diagnostic analysis of children's fundamental motor skills of running, jumping, throwing, catching, kicking and hitting. In the guidance, each skill is divided into its constituent components, termed 'performance criteria' and stages, by age, are allocated to each performance criterion. The sequence in which each of the components normally appears is also shown. The trainees learnt to observe closely, to match performances to the guidance and by the end of the course, could spot levels of competence, make comparisons and give useful teaching points for improvement.

By the age of 5 years (QCA 2000), children are expected to be able to:

- move with confidence, imagination and in safety
- move with control and coordination
- travel around, under, over and through balancing and climbing equipment
- show awareness of space, of themselves and of others
- recognize the importance of keeping healthy and recognize changes that happen to their bodies when they are active
- use a range of small and large equipment and handle tools, objects, construction and malleable materials safely and with increasing control.

The roles of the teacher, then, are to:

- plan challenging physical activities that build on existing experience and develop ability, confidence and self-esteem
- provide sufficient movement experience to meet the learning needs of each child, including those with delayed movement development
- target appropriate intervention to help the learners as needed
- provide a safe and supportive environment
- provide indoor and outdoor space with appropriate equipment for motor skill development
- set up activities that are enjoyable, imaginative, well planned and allow too for free play.

Teaching 5–11-year-olds

'To see young people growing in physical skills, self-confidence and self-worth is a truly enriching experience. Nowhere in school is it more visible than in PE' (DfEE 1999: 128). 'Through the movement experience offered within Physical Education we engage the affective, interpersonal and cognitive dimensions of the child' (Douglas 1999: 2). She goes on to suggest that movement is also the integrating element of all of these. In our planning and teaching of PE we therefore need to keep all these dimensions in mind as we incorporate them alongside the elements that make up the Attainment Target for Physical Education in Curriculum 2000 (DfEE 1999).

For children aged 5–7 years, teaching should include opportunities to:

- explore, copy, repeat and remember skills
- develop coordination and control
- link skills and learn about composition and tactics
- describe and comment on their own and others' work
- improve performance
- understand safe exercise and health-related aspects of physical activity.

For children aged 7–11 years, teaching should include opportunities to:

- select and combine skills, techniques and ideas appropriately, accurately and consistently

- modify and refine skills, techniques, tactics and compositions with precision, control and fluency, in response to changing circumstances
- improve their own and others' performance
- explain the effects of exercise and how to prepare for and recover from exercise
- explain safety, fitness and health.

Summary

Physical education, to be effective in fulfilling its educative role, should provide children with enhancement of their physical and motor development and coordination, along with extension of their movement vocabulary and skill and the language to communicate that learning. The curriculum should challenge the emerging physical, intellectual, aesthetic and emotional abilities of the child. It should initiate children into some of the socially recognized sports and recreation of our culture. The physical education programme must also contribute to children's knowledge and understanding of the requirement to take personal responsibility for developing and maintaining a healthy, active and safe lifestyle.

Questions to ask

1 What are the skills, knowledge and understanding necessary for the children in your school, class or setting to become physically educated?
2 How could your provision for children's physical education be developed in relation to resources, time and planning?
3 Could new partnerships be established to enhance your children's opportunities to access a broad, balanced physical education curriculum?
4 What are the new challenges for teachers of physical education today, in order to raise standards of physical education learning and achievement for children?

6

Physical literacy, active learning and active teaching

Cameo 1

A group of children, aged 10 and 11 years, arrive in the hall from their classrooms at the start of morning break. One brings the tape recorder and another the audio-tape, to play the music that they have selected and agreed as best suited to accompany their dance. Within two minutes they have cleared a space in which to work, organized themselves into two rows and started to practise their group dance. The back row dancers check the accuracy and expressiveness of their footwork, posture, body and arm actions through observation of the front row dancers and they swop over to double-check. Between performances, they discuss together and peer tutor one another to fine tune the content and improve the rhythm, spatial qualities and fluency of their dance. They communicate high levels of motivation, autonomy, independence and pleasure in their learning and they undertake high levels of physical activity in a short time. Their teachers recognize the quality of these achievements, commending the children's ability to work cooperatively whenever they meet together, with full commitment and concentration and without teacher intervention.

Cameo 2

Adam (aged 10) is keen to take up ice-hockey. In the mean-time he has learnt to roller-blade and has now progressed to roller hockey. In Figure 6.1 he shows his expertise.

Figure 6.1   Adam (aged 10) practising roller-blade hockey

Cameo 3

The subject leader for PE in a primary school discusses with colleagues how best to use the combined expertise of staff to provide every child with the best available PE curriculum. They maximize the timetable slots, both within and outside curriculum time, throughout the week, to make the most of the school's excellent facilities for PE and they discuss how to develop children's thinking skills as well as their knowledge, understanding and performance in PE.

Introduction

In this chapter the concept of physical literacy is explored in the contexts of the child as an active learner, teachers as active practitioners and school and curriculum as providing active contexts. The significance of physical literacy is considered as an integral part of the education of the whole child, being made up of a wide range of 'Intelligences', with reference to Howard Gardner's 'seven intelligences' (Gardner 1993b) as the backdrop to this holistic approach. Issues for the teacher include educating children's

Figure 6.2 Concentrating on playing the steel pans

'bodily kinaesthetic intelligence', empowering children to take responsibility for their own learning and seeing their present learning as stepping stones to future achievements. Above all, the teacher's role is proposed as enabling children to become physically literate.

The contexts for active teaching and learning include those environments and curricula which offer challenge and progression and which prepare children for the opportunities and demands of this new millennium.

The child

Intelligence seems most commonly to be assessed according to academic ability. However Gardner (1993b) proposes that people possess seven forms of intelligence, each of which contributes to the ways in which they learn, gain understanding of the world and demonstrate their overall profile of intelligence. Of these forms of intelligence, the two that are currently given the most attention in British schools are those related to language and mathematics, namely linguistic and logico-mathematical intelligences.

These are allocated the majority of the curriculum time in English primary schools at the turn of the century and teaching in all curriculum subjects also paid attention to the opportunities available to develop both numeracy skills and skills in language (speaking, listening, reading and writing). However, Gardner defines another five significant domains, which together make up the intelligent person. These are the musical, spatial and bodily kinaesthetic intelligences and two forms of personal intelligence, one related to understanding of others (interpersonal), and the other related to the understanding of ourselves (intrapersonal). He proposes that children should be enhanced and taught across each of the seven domains of intelligence and that assessment should provide evidence for achievement across the entire profile. Children will differ in the relative strength of each intelligence domain and in the ways in which each domain is developed and combined with others in order to carry out tasks, solve problems and learn. Consider the range of intelligences involved in playing the steel pans. The children shown here involve their bodily-kinaesthetic intelligence, using the fine motor skills of their hands as well as their musical, mathematical and spatial intelligences to contribute to successful performance by the whole group.

Bodily kinaesthetic intelligence is seen as 'the ability to use one's body in highly differentiated and skilled ways, for expressive as well as goal-directed purposes' (Gardner 1993a: 207). Control of whole body movement, such as is required by dancers, who communicate through expressive movement, or by swimmers, whose movement has a goal-directed purpose, is thus an example of bodily kinaesthetic intelligence. Another characteristic is 'the capacity to work skilfully with objects, both those that involve the fine motor movements of one's fingers and those that exploit gross motor movements of the body' (Gardner 1993a: 207). Bodily kinaesthetic intelligence is thus essential for surgeons, dentists and keyboard workers, for example, where fine motor control is crucial, whereas for cellists, parachutists and tennis players, for example, whole and fine motor control are combined for successful performance. Further characteristics of bodily kinaesthetic intelligence include an acute sense of timing, an ability to anticipate the end product, to pick up relevant signals from the environment and from within the body and brain as appropriate. Here we see that bodily intelligence cannot be separated from thinking skills. This concept will be explored later in the chapter.

In the meantime, how does Gardner's bodily kinaesthetic intelligence relate to his other intelligence domains and how do his multiple intelligences relate to physical literacy? An answer to the first question, taking musical intelligence as the example, is that children draw on and develop their musical intelligence whenever they engage in physical activities requiring rhythm, timing, composition and stimuli provided by the myriad of sounds and forms of music. The most common example of exploiting musical intelligence within bodily intelligence is in dance. Children's spatial intelligence is educated and incorporated into their bodily intelligence as they learn to observe and copy movement, to manage their bodies within their personal space (the icosohedron of space always surrounding the body) and within the general space of the working environment, shared by all movers. Children also use their spatial intelligence as they develop the locational aspects of their movement memory. Spatial intelligence is dependent on bodily intelligence in the fine motor functioning required for drawing, painting and sculpture and is deployed during orienteering activities, for example, when learners translate the spatial representation of a map into planned activity in order to reach a checkpoint on a trail.

The children in Cameo 1 display aspects of their bodily kinaesthetic intelligence as they practise their dance; their linguistic intelligence as they peer tutor and discuss the work in progress; their mathematical and spatial intelligences as they use number and space in the composition of the dance; their musical intelligence in relation to the choice and use of the accompanying music; they also draw on their personal and interpersonal intelligences, as they work on the relationships between themselves, other individuals and the group in creating the choreography, peer tutoring and in performing the dance. In this aspect of their learning and at this stage in their development these children not only are active learners, but also have exposed themselves to all of Gardner's domains of intelligence and have attained high levels of achievement at this stage in their education.

The concept of mind and body synchrony (discussed earlier) was at its height in the Classical era, when the Greeks sought harmony between mind and body, by training the mind to enable the body to move with mastery. The ability to translate thinking into action is still essential for the achievement of bodily kinaesthetic intelligence, demonstrating that the 'physical' and the 'mental' cannot be divorced from one another. Gardner states: 'One should look upon mental activity as a means to the end of executing actions' (1993a: 211). He goes on to describe the complexity of the movement system, calling as it does on 'a dizzying variety of neural and muscular components in a highly differentiated and integrated fashion'. These include the mechanisms in the brain that provide for the gaining of feedback (information about an action or part of that action), by comparing the intended outcome with the current action, so that movement can be continually refined and regulated. This neatly reinforces the importance of the integration of mind, body and environment, which is the main theme of Clark (1996), when he writes about putting mind, body and world together again. Clearly, Clark sees the person as being made up of mind and body, linked in their function to operate within the world. He says: 'Cognitive development cannot usefully be treated in isolation from issues concerning the child's physical embedding in the world' (1997: 36). Clark speaks of the mind, body and world as 'equal partners' in the construction of 'robust, flexible behaviours' (1997: 45). His analogy of the mind as a 'leaky organ, forever escaping its natural confines and mingling shamelessly with body and with world' (1997: 53) nicely conjures up, for me, a picture of the interplay of the three partners involved in the child's process of exploring physical literacy. Clark also speaks of 'brain–body coalitions embedded in ecologically realistic environments' (1997: 98).

The physically active child then, operates in the three aspects of body, mind and world, all at the same time and, in working towards physical literacy, explores relevant aspects of all seven of Gardner's intelligences.

The teacher

As the Teacher Training Agency (TTA 1998a: 1) reminds us: 'Teaching is without doubt the most important profession; without teaching there would be no other professions. It is also the most rewarding. What role in society can be more crucial than that which shapes children's lives and prepares them for adulthood?' The TTA has adopted the slogan 'No one forgets a good teacher' and more often than not this is true in physical education, where, because the learning is so public, the teacher can have a profound influence on the learner, for worse and more often for better. The active teacher can unlock the potential of every child, can develop children's talents and build on strengths, can help them to show initiative, think and talk about and take responsibility for their learning and show initiative, so that children flourish in their journey towards physical literacy.

In recent years, concern has been expressed about the lack of involvement by children in physical activity and health-related exercise. Some of the categories of physical activity that are proposed by Armstrong (1996: 100) remind us of the importance of ensuring that we as teachers provide children with significant learning and experience of exercise for the body. Such activity should involve locomotion in which the weight of the body is carried over distance, to help prevent overweight and obesity and to ensure the development of a strong bone structure. He also proposes activity for the heart in which levels of intensity optimally stress the cardiovascular system and help children to develop fitter hearts, muscles and oxygen delivery systems. Research with primary school children in England by Armstrong and Bray produced results which showed that 'children rarely engage in amounts of sustained activity of sufficient intensity to optimise their aerobic fitness' (Armstrong 1996: 101). Given the reported decline in extracurricular school sport during the 1990s and the reduced physical education curriculum time in England, which was found to be less than almost all other European countries at the turn of the century, there seemed to be a serious threat to health-enhancing activity.

In one study, over one-third of the boys and half the girls did not experience even one sustained ten-minute period of moderate intensity physical activity each week. If perpetuated, this may have important consequences for the future health of the next generation and has certainly exercised the minds of curriculum planners at the start of the twenty-first century. In Curriculum 2000 there is a brief but highly significant statement early in the document (DfEE 1999: 16): 'The government believes that two hours of physical activity a week, including the national curriculum for physical education and extra-curricular activities, should be an aspiration for all schools.'

Armstrong (1996) goes on to outline some psychological benefits of physical activity, including that of stimulating a sense of well-being, reducing anxiety and stress and improving self-confidence and self-esteem. While some children relish the competitive team-game-type of activity, others enjoy aspects of the wide range of individual sports and recreations such as cycling, skateboarding, swimming, walking, gymnastics, dance or aerobics. In Cameo 2, Adam has discovered the potential of roller-blading, both as a fun activity in itself now and as providing preparatory learning for ice-hockey. He does not seem to need adult guidance to promote his interest in physical activity and he readily demonstrates self-motivation in activities that provide both exercise and challenge. However, in thinking about activity for life generally, Armstrong suggests that 'the way exercise is presented to children may have important implications for future activity patterns and consequently for their health and well-being as adults' (Armstrong 1996: 109).

Teachers can help children to enjoy participating in the range of curricular and extra-curricular physical education activities available in school, perhaps through adopting a variety of teaching styles, ranging from direct instructional teaching at one end of the spectrum of styles, to leading pupils in a discovery approach to their learning. Recognizing and attending to children's learning styles can greatly enhance opportunities, particularly for children who need extra encouragement to develop their self-motivation for physical education. Discovering preferences and making informed choices for active participation in physical activities in adulthood must be established in childhood. Maintenance of the benefits of health-related exercise relies on continued participation and therefore children's PE experience between the ages of 5 and 11 years must be designed to make a positive impact on their choices as they proceed through primary school and into secondary education at the age of 11 years.

Gardner proposes that each child's intelligence profile can be assessed and that it is then possible for 'each child to be aligned with curriculum, particularly the way in which that curriculum is presented to the child' (Gardner 1993a: xix) in order to enhance the child's educational opportunities and options (Gardner 1993a: 9).

A concern at the turn of the century in England was to find ways within short initial teacher training (ITT) courses to prepare to teach physical education. Trainees used their learning from the taught course as a springboard for continued initial training in school placements, by working alongside the PE subject leader. This integrated approach to ITT proved to be invaluable in settings where specialist support was available within placement schools. Other schools have tackled the problem of teachers' lack of subject knowledge by developing the role of the subject leader as described in the TTA *National Standards for Subject Leaders* (TTA 1998b: 6, 7). These have been interpreted for PE and published in the document *Achieving Excellence: Subject Leader in Physical Education* by the British Association of Advisers and Lecturers in Physical Education (BAALPE 1999b: 8, 9, 16). For example, subject leaders are charged with providing a broad balanced curriculum, with ensuring quality PE, with providing relevant guidance, staff training opportunities and with enabling colleagues to teach to their strengths. This approach was supported by David Hargreaves, who suggested that teachers' peers are the most credible source of new knowledge and how to apply it (in Woodhead 1999: 9). Woodhead goes on to suggest the following problem-solving strategy adopted by teachers: 'Teachers naturally "tinker" to discover what works best and in so doing they creatively search for, and test out, the solutions to problems' (Woodhead 1999: section 22).

The context

'Physical Education and Sport are a fundamental part of the education of all young people' (Department for Culture, Media and Sport (DCMS) 2000: 7); 'excellent physical education and school sport are a key part of an effective school and PE is an essential part of a broad balanced curriculum' (DCMS 2000: 8). These are strong and supportive statements about the importance of physical education in the new millennium and the Department for Culture, Media and Sport in England has 'nailed its colours to the mast' in determining to improve provision for physical education and sport. In tackling the shortfall of qualified physical education teachers in primary schools, government policy focused on ways to raise standards in physical education. These include commitment to improved teacher education, to the provision of a subject leader for groups of schools, 'who will be trained and supported to raise standards' and to making available £160 million to support out-of-school learning, including encouraging schools to provide a range of after-school physical education and sport activities for all pupils, whatever their age or ability (DCMS 2000: 31). This commitment provides for the introduction of a real change in provision for children and for enhancing positive attitudes towards participation in physical activity for all pupils.

The context for such change is the active school. What is an active school? I suggest that the staff described in Cameo 3 work in an active school. Theirs is a school with a policy for the promotion of physical activity, which directly addresses children's activity levels and which raises awareness, sets high expectations, develops expertise, confidence and positive attitudes, to ensure that all children can catch the habit of a lifetime – to maintain an active lifestyle after leaving the school. They work towards a high quality, broad and balanced PE curriculum, inclusive of all children. With limited time and resources and many pressing priorities, what are the quality physical education opportunities offered by your school to the children?

Is yours an active school, with active teachers and active children? Are you facilitated in making whatever changes are necessary to keep abreast of developments in physical education and to take up new opportunities for enhancing teaching and learning? For example, has your school been able to invest in the latest audio-visual aids, such as a digital camera to capture and make still photos of pupil learning in physical education or PowerPoint and other computer programs that can provide interactive movement teaching opportunities? Do children in your school use a video camera to record their movement and gain feedback on their performance and can they access a library of video and CD-ROM material to see models for their movement learning? Has your school a big screen to use with video of a dance, for example, to help children to 'match a model' and to learn new movement vocabulary as a basis for their own movement exploration and further choreographic activity?

For those who work with children aged 3–5 years the Qualifications and Curriculum Agency in England set out curriculum guidance on effective teaching and learning (QCA 2000). Early years practitioners are given guidance on planning and teaching an appropriate curriculum in six areas, including personal, social and emotional development; communication, language and literacy; mathematical development; knowledge and understanding of the world; physical development; creative development. While each of the other five areas of development call to a greater or lesser extent on the ability of children to use movement competently and confidently, the physical development area focuses on the six movement-orientated early learning goals described in Chapter 5.

Adopting these early learning goals can effectively set the parameters for launching children into a rich and challenging physical education curriculum for children aged 5–11 years, in which teachers foster and facilitate the achievement of physical literacy.

Summary

Understanding that children display a varied profile of abilities across a wide range of intelligences provides the springboard for active teachers to educate children in physical literacy. Helping children to discover their strengths in this area can enormously increase their confidence, self-esteem, achievement and pleasure in physical education.

Questions to ask

1 What is it to be physically literate?
2 In what ways can the children with whom you work achieve a greater measure of physical literacy?
3 What more could be developed in your class or setting to provide appropriately active contexts and to ensure active teaching and active learning?

 Conclusion

In 1991, the United Kingdom Sports Council stated in a promotional leaflet: 'Physical literacy creates literacy in movement, which is as vital to every person as literacy in verbal expression itself.' The sentiment expressed in this statement very much recognizes the centrality of physical competence to human performance. However, the statement, made at the start of the 1990s, has sparked a debate that will probably span the next decade, since, as yet, there is no single definition of physical literacy and no text that adequately explains what it is to be physically literate.

Within the current debate, then, the question remains: 'What is physical literacy?' I would conjecture that for each child physical literacy is both a process of ongoing change and a product or series of summative stages. It seems to me that physical literacy is the sum of movement achievements at and between each stage in the child's growth and development and involves the totality of experience, knowledge and understanding of movement and its applications for functional and expressive performance of parts of, or the whole of an action or series of actions. It seems to me that children's physical literacy changes over time as bodily capacities change and as mind–body–world knowledge and experience increase. Physical literacy would seem to incorporate all seven of Gardner's 'intelligences', as appropriate. To be physically literate will be to have achieved a perfect balance of these in whatever movement situation prevails or is planned for future action.

Questions that remain for further investigation include:

1 Is physical literacy a child's optimum physical development and movement achievement put together, or are there other components?
2 Does physical literacy involve all the child's knowledge understanding and experience of movement gained through play, through daily movement experience and through physical education opportunities, or are there other dimensions?
3 How far can physical children who are also active learners invest in their own physical literacy? What is the role of the active teacher in accommodating the many relevant changes that occur, with seeming relentlessness, in education, society and culture in order to promote physical literacy?
4 What contexts are instrumental in making up the entitlement for children who are working towards becoming physically literate?

This book was intentionally subtitled 'Investigating physical literacy', in order to open up the debate, to seek for answers to the questions above and to challenge readers to continue to search for a definition and to give the children with whom they work every opportunity to reach their potential to become physically literate.

Best wishes to you for success in your journey into children's physical literacy!

Bibliography

Alldridge, D. and Fisher, R. (1994) *Active PE*. Hemel Hempstead: Simon & Schuster.

Armstrong, N. (1996) *New Directions in Physical Education*. London: Cassell.

Armstrong, N. and Welsman, J. (1997) *Young People and Physical Activity*. Oxford: Oxford University Press.

Arnold, P. (1970) *Education, Physical Education and Personality Development*. London: Heinemann.

Arts Council of Great Britain (1993) *Arts in Education*.

Asher, J. (1983) *Learning Another Language through Actions*. Los Angeles: Sky Oaks.

Assessment of Performance Unit (1983) *Physical Development*. London: Department of Education and Science.

Aussie Sport (1991) *Sport Start*. Melbourne: Australian Sports Commission.

BAALPE (1999a) *Safe Practice in Physical Education*. Dudley: Dudley LEA.

BAALPE (1999b) *Achieving Excellence: Subject Leader in Physical Education*. Dudley: Dudley LEA.

Barter, M. (1999a) Positive thinking, *PE and Sport Today*, 1 (winter). Birmingham: Questions Publishing.

Barter, M. (1999b) Squeeze it in, *PE and Sport Today*, 1 (winter). Birmingham: Questions Publishing.

Bearne, E. (ed.) (1998) *Use of Language across the Primary Curriculum*. London: Routledge.

Beetlestone, F. (1998) *Creative Children, Imaginative Teaching*. Buckingham: Open University Press.

Bennett, N., Wood, L. and Rogers, S. (1996) *Teaching through Play*. Buckingham: Open University Press.

Berk, L. (1996) *Infants, Children and Adolescents*. Boston, MA: Allyn and Bacon.

Best, D. (1985) *Feeling and Reason in the Arts*. London: Allen & Unwin.

Biddle, S., Sallis, J. and Cavill, N. (eds) (1998) *Young and Active*. London: Health Education Authority.

Blake, B. (1996) *Use of Language within the National Curriculum for Physical Education*. Nafferton: BAALPE (British Association of Advisers and Lecturers in Physical Education).

Blake, B. (1999) Citizen sport, *PE and Sport Today*, 1 (winter). Birmingham: Questions Publishing.

Board of Education (1933) *Syllabus for Physical Training for Schools 1933*. London: HMSO.

Boorman, P. (1998) Make the right moves, *Nursery World*, 2 April.

Bourne, J. (ed.) (1994) *Thinking through Primary Practice*. London: Routledge.

Brinson, P. (1991) *Dance as Education*. London: Falmer Press.

Bruce, T. (1991) *Time to Play: In Early Childhood Education*. London: Hodder & Stoughton Educational.

Bruner, J. (1983) *Child's Talk: Learning to Use Language*. Oxford: Oxford University Press.

Burton, A. and Miller, D. (1998) *Movement Skill Assessment*. Champaign, IL: Human Kinetics.

Casbon, C. (1999) Curriculum 2000 New Orders, *PE and Sport Today*, 1 (winter). Birmingham: Questions Publishing.

Clark, A. (1996) *Putting Brain, Body and World Together*. Cambridge, MA: MIT Press.

Cowley, T. (1998) *Balancing Act: A Motor-learning Game*. San Antonio, TX: Therapy Skill Builders.

Crace, J. (2000) Literacy 2, Sport 0, *Guardian Education*, 29 February.

Craig, G. (1995) *Children Today*. Englewood Cliffs, NJ: Prentice-Hall.

Cratty, B. (1986) *Perceptual and Motor Development in Infants and Children*. Englewood Cliffs, NJ: Prentice-Hall.

Curtis, J. (1997) *Physical Activity in Human Experience*. Champaign, IL: Human Kinetics.

Dane, R. (1978) *The Poetry of the Lakes*. Darlington: Nordales.

David, T. (ed.) (1999) *Young Children Learning*. London: Paul Chapman.

Davis, G. (1971) *Training Creative Thinking*. New York: Holt, Rinehart & Winston.

Dean, J. (1999) *Improving the Primary School*. London: Routledge.

de Bono, E. (1972) *Children Solve Problems*. Harmondsworth: Penguin.

de Bóo, M. (1999) *Enquiring Children, Challenging Teaching*. Buckingham: Open University Press.

Department for Culture, Media and Sport (DCMS) (1999) *All Our Futures: Creativity, Culture and Education*. London: DCMS.

Department for Culture, Media and Sport (DCMS) (2000) *A Sporting Future for All*. London: DCMS.

Department for Education and Employment (DfEE) (1997a) *Excellence in Schools.* London: HMSO.

Department for Education and Employment (DfEE) (1997b) *From Targets to Action.* London: HMSO.

Department for Education and Employment (DfEE) (1998) *Teaching: High Status, High Standards.* London: HMSO.

Department for Education and Employment (DfEE) (1999) *The National Curriculum for England and Wales.* London: QCA.

Department of Education and Science (DES) (1972) *Movement.* London: HMSO.

Department of Education and Science (DES) (1990) *Interim Report of the DES National Curriculum Physical Education Working Party.* London: HMSO.

Department of Education, Victoria (1996) *Fundamental Motor Skills.* Melbourne: State of Victoria.

DES Task Group on Assessment and Testing (1988) *National Curriculum.* London: HMSO.

Douglas, M. (1999) *Dance.* London: Hodder & Stoughton.

Drummond, M.J. (1993) *Assessing Children's Learning.* London: David Fulton.

Eisner (1972) *Educating Artistic Vision.* London: Macmillan.

Elkington, H. (1998) *Swimming.* London: Hodder & Stoughton.

Eriksen, A. (1985) *Playground Design.* New York: Van Nostrand Reinhold.

Fullan, M. (1982) *The Meaning of Educational Change.* Toronto: Ontario Institute for Studies in Education (OISE).

Fullan, M. (1991) *The New Meaning of Educational Change.* London: Cassell.

Gallahue, D.L. (1989) *Understanding Motor Development*, 2nd edn. Dubuque: WCB Brown and Benchmark.

Gallahue, D. (1996) *Developmental Physical Education for Today's Children.* Madison, WI: Brown & Benchmark.

Gallahue, D. and Ozmun, J. (1995) *Understanding Motor Development*, 3rd edn. Madison, WI: Brown & Benchmark.

Gardner, H. (1991) *The Unschooled Mind.* New York: Basic Books.

Gardner, H. (1993a) *Frames of Mind.* London: Fontana.

Gardner, H. (1993b) *Multiple Intelligences.* New York: Basic Books.

Gildenhuys, C. (1996) Movement and second language acquisition, *Sport, Education and Society*, 1(2): 12–16.

Goddard Blyth, S. (2000) First steps to the most important ABC, *Times Educational Supplement*, 7 January.

Graham, G. (1993) *Children Moving.* Palo Alto, CA: Mayfield.

Hagger, M. (1999) *Coaching Young Performers.* Leeds: National Coaching Foundation.

Haigh, G. (1999) Walk on the wild side, *Times Educational Supplement Primary*, 22 January.

Haldy, M. and Haack, L. (1995) *Making It Easy: Sensorimotor Activities at Home and School.* San Antonio, TX: Therapy Skill Builders.

Hallam, S. (1998) *Instrumental Teaching*. Oxford: Heinemann.

Hans, J. (1981) *The Play of the World*. Cambridge, MA: University of Massachusetts Press.

Hayes, D. (1999) *Planning, Teaching and Class Management in Primary Schools*. London: David Fulton.

Haywood, K. (1993a) *Life Span Motor Development*. Champaign, IL: Human Kinetics.

Haywood, K. (1993b) *Laboratory Activities for Life Span Motor Development*. Champaign, IL: Human Kinetics.

Health Education Authority (HEA) (1996) *Getting Active*. London: HEA.

Health Education Authority (HEA) (1997) *Young People and Physical Activity*. London: HEA.

Health Education Authority (HEA) (1998) *Young and Active?* London: HEA.

Hendy, L. and Whitebread, D. (1999) Interpretations of independent learning in the early years. Paper presented to Third International Early Years Conference, Warwick, 12–16 April.

Hereford and Worcester County Council (1992) *Inspection Advice and Training Service Physical Education Guidelines*. Worcester: Hereford and Worcester County Council.

Hobart, C. and Frankel, J. (1995) *A Practical Guide to Child Observation*. Cheltenham: Stanley Thornes.

Homerton College PE Department (1998) *Teaching Primary Physical Education*. Cambridge: Homerton College.

Hughes, F. (1999) *Children, Play and Development*. Boston, MA: Allyn and Bacon.

Hunt, M. (1995) *Learning to Move, Moving to Learn*. Worcester: Hereford and Worcester County Council.

Hurst, V. and Joseph, J. (1998) *Supporting Early Learning*. Buckingham: Open University Press.

Kelly, J. (1998) Let creativity shape the future, *Times Educational Supplement*, 27 February.

Kitson, N. and Spibey, I. (1997) *Drama 7–11: Developing Primary Teaching Skills*. London: Routledge.

Laszlo, J. and Van Rossum, J. (1994) *Motor Development*. Amsterdam: VU Uitgeverij.

Lee, C. (1984) *The Growth and Development of Children*. London: Longman.

Logsdon, B. (1984) *Physical Education for Children: A Focus on the Teaching Process*. Philadelphia, PA: Lea & Febiger.

Martens, R. (1975) *Social Psychology and Physical Activity*. New York: Harper & Row.

Martens, R. (1990) *Successful Coaching*. Champaign, IL: Human Kinetics.

Maude, P. (1994) *The Gym Kit* (video and handbook), Albion Television, Health Promotion Research Trust. Cambridge: Homerton College.

Maude, P. (1996a) Differentiation in physical education, in E. Bearne (ed.) *Differentiation and Diversity in the Primary School*. London: Routledge.

Maude, P. (1996b) From movement development into early years physical education, in D. Whitebread (ed.) *Teaching and Learning in the Early Years*. London: Routledge.

Maude, P. (1997) *Gymnastics*. London: Hodder & Stoughton.

Maude, P. (1998) I like climing, hoping and biking: the language of physical education, in E. Bearne (ed.) *Use of Language across the Curriculum*. London: Routledge.

Merry, R. (1998) *Successful Children, Successful Teaching*. Buckingham: Open University Press.

Ministry of Education (1952) *Moving and Growing*. London: HMSO.

Ministry of Education (1953) *Planning the Programme*. London: HMSO.

Mitsuru, S. (1992) *Design of Children's Play Environments*. New York: McGraw-Hill.

Morris, D. (1969) *The Human Zoo*. Toronto: Clarke, Irwin.

Moyles, J. (ed.) (1989) *Just Playing?* Milton Keynes: Open University Press.

Moyles, J. (ed.) (1994) *The Excellence of Play*. Buckingham: Open University Press.

National Advisory Committee on Creative and Cultural Education (1999) *All our Futures*. London: DfEE.

Nisbet, J. and Shucksmith, J. (1986) *Learning Strategies*. London: Routledge & Kegan Paul.

Noren-Bjorn, E. (1982) *The Impossible Playground*. New York: Leisure Press.

Noren-Bjorn, E. (1997) *The Impossible Playground*. New York: Leisure Press.

Nostrand, A. (1985) *Playground Design*. New York: Van Nostrand.

Ofsted (1995) *Guidance on the Inspection of Nursery and Primary Schools*. London: HMSO.

Ofsted (1996a) *Physical Education and Sport in Schools*. London: HMSO.

Ofsted (1996b) *Primary Subject Guidance*. London: HMSO.

Ofsted (1996c) *Physical Education and Sport in Schools: A Survey of Good Practice*. London: HMSO.

Opie, I. and Opie, P. (1969) *Children's Games in Street and Playground*. Oxford: Oxford University Press.

Orlick, T. (1998) *Embracing your Potential*. Champaign, IL: Human Kinetics.

Owens, K. (1993) *The World of the Child*. New York: Macmillan.

Papert, S. (1980) *Mindstorms: Children, Computers and Powerful Ideas*. Brighton: Harvester.

Qualifications and Curriculum Authority (QCA) (1998) *Maintaining Breadth and Balance*. London: QCA.

Qualifications and Curriculum Authority (QCA) (1999a) *Early Learning Goals*. London: QCA.

Qualifications and Curriculum Authority (QCA) (1999b) *Terminology in Physical Education*. London: QCA.

Qualifications and Curriculum Authority (QCA) (2000) *Curriculum Guidance for the Foundation Stage*. London: QCA.

Rasch, P. (1971) *Applied Anatomy*. Philadelphia, PA: Lea & Febiger.

Rathus, S. (1988) *Understanding Child Development*. New York: Holt, Rinehart and Winston.

Raymond, C. (1998) *Co-ordinating Physical Education across the Primary School*. London: Falmer.

Ripley, K., Daines, B. and Barrett, J. (1997) *Dyspraxia: A Guide for Parents and Teachers*. London: David Fulton.

Saach, C. (1988) *Childhood Play*. New York: New York Press.

Santrock, J. (1993) *Children*. Madison, WI: Brown & Benchmark.

Saul, R. (1988) *Persons, Minds and Bodies*. Ontario: University Press of Ontario.

Schickedanz, J. (1990) *Understanding Children*. Palo Alto, CA: Mayfield.

Schmidt, R. (1991) *Motor Learning and Performance*. Champaign, IL: Human Kinetics.

School Curriculum and Assessment Authority (SCAA) (1997) *Physical Education and the Use of Language*. Hayes: SCAA.

SCAA/QCA (1997) *Looking at Children's Learning: Desirable Outcomes for Children's Learning on Entering Compulsory Education*. London: DfEE.

School Examination and Assessment Council (1991) *Records of Achievement in Primary Schools*. London: HMSO.

Slade, P. (1995) *Child Play*. London: Jessica Kingsley.

Smith, J. (1999) The People's PE, *PE and Sport Today*, 1 (winter). Birmingham: Questions Publishing.

Standards and Effectiveness Unit (1997) *From Targets to Action*. London: DfEE.

Stewart, D. (1990) *The Right to Movement*. London: Falmer.

Sutton-Smith, B. (1986) *Toys as Culture*. New York: Gardner.

Teacher Training Agency (TTA) (1998a) *Teaching: A Guide to Becoming a Better Teacher*. Chelmsford: TTA.

Teacher Training Agency (TTA) (1998b) *National Standards for Subject Leaders*. Chelmsford: TTA.

Thomas, J. (1984) *Motor Development during Childhood and Adolescence*. Minneapolis, MN: Burgess.

Thomas Coram Institute (1991) *Children's Play*. London: Thomas Coram Institute.

Wall, J. and Murray, N. (1990) *Children and Movement*. Dubuque, IA: Wm C. Brown.

Wesson, K., Wiggins, N., Thompson, G. and Hartigan, S. (1998) *Sport and PE*. London: Hodder & Stoughton.

Wetton, P. (1988) *Physical Education in the Nursery and Infant School*. London: Croom Helm.

Wetton, P. (1999) Physical education in the early years, in *Primary PE Focus*, summer. Reading: PEA UK.

Whitebread, D. (ed.) (1996) *Teaching and Learning in the Early Years.* London: Routledge.

Williams, A. (ed.) (2000) *Primary School Physical Education.* London: Routledge Falmer.

Woodhead, M. (ed.) (1991) *Growing up in a Changing Society.* London: Routledge.

Wragg, E. (ed.) (1984) *Classroom Teaching Skills.* London: Routledge.

Wragg, E. (ed.) (1993a) *An Introduction to Classroom Observation.* London: Routledge.

Wragg, E. (ed.) (1993b) *Primary Teaching Skills.* London: Routledge.

Wright, H. and Sugden, D. (1999) *Physical Education for All.* London: David Fulton.

Zion, L. (1994) *The Physical Side of Learning.* Byron, CA: Front Row Experience.

Index